# Developmental Signatures

Core Values and Practices in Waldorf Education
for Children Ages 3–9

# Developmental Signatures

## Core Values and Practices in Waldorf Education for Children Ages 3–9

by

Rainer Patzlaff
Wolfgang Sassmannshausen
et al.

*Printed with support from the Waldorf Curriculum Fund
and the Waldorf Schools Fund*

Published by:
Waldorf Publications at the
Research Institute for Waldorf Education

Title: *Developmental Signatures:
Core Values and Practices in Waldorf Education for Children Ages 3–9*
Authors: Rainer Patzlaff, Wolfgang Sassmannshausen, et al.
Translator: Karin DiGiacomo
Editor: David Mitchell
Proofreader: Ann Erwin
Cover: Hallie Wootan
Cover Photograph: Carla Cummings

First edition © 2007 by AWSNA
ISBN # 978-1-888365-81-8

Second edition © 2016 by Waldorf Publications
ISBN #978-1-936367-96-2

A joint collaboration of the
Waldorf Early Childhood Association of North America (WECAN),
AWSNA Publications, and the Research Institute for Waldorf Education

Originally published as two separate volumes in German by the
Pedagogical Research Center of the Association of Waldorf Schools in Germany
in 2005 and 2006
  *Leitlinien der Waldorfpädagogik für die Altersstufe von 3 bis 9 Jahren: Teil I*
    by Rainer Patzlaff and Wolfgang Sassmannshausen
    First printed by the Pädagogische Forschungsstelle in Stuttgart, Germany
    ISBN # 978-3-927786-93-1
  *Leitlinien der Waldorfpädagogik für die Altersstufe von 3 bis 9 Jahren: Teil II*
    by Telse Kardel, Claudia McKeen, Martyn Rawson, Wolfgang
    Sassmannshausen and others
    ISBN # 978-3-927286-65-8
Commissioned by the German Association of Waldorf Schools and the
International Association of Waldorf Kindergartens
Translated with permission.

# Contents

From the Editor .................................................. 11

Foreword ........................................................ 13
    by Susan Howard

### Part 1

### Waldorf Education for Children: Ages Three to Nine

Introduction .................................................... 17
    by Rainer Patzlaff and Wolfgang Sassmannshausen

At the Center, the Individuality ................................ 19
    Steps on the Way to Human Freedom
    Education and Self-Education of the Child
    The Physical, Vital, and Mental Instruments of the "I"
    Salutogenesis as a Foundation for the Educational Process
    Developing a Healthy Physical Organization
    Developing a Sense of Coherence through Direct Experience
    Development of Resilience

Early Childhood Learning and Its Conditions .................... 28
    The Special Nature of Early Childhood Learning
    The Pedagogy of Creating an Environment: Order and Reliability
    The Pedagogy of Creating an Environment: Rhythm and Repetition
    Creating a Learning Environment: Facts and Connections
    The Personality of the Teacher/Parent as a Formative Influence
        on the Child
    Self-Education of the Educators
    The Significance of Free Play

The Transition to Elementary School Learning:
When Is the Right Time? ........................................ 39
    Play and Social Behavior of the Six-Year-Old
    Intellectual Precocity and Dissociation
    The Seven-Year Rhythm—A Health-Generating Principle
    The Metamorphosis of the Forces Shaping the Body
    The Launch of the Faculty of Imagination

The First School Year................................... 49
    From Implicit to Explicit Learning
    Learning in an Atmosphere of Soul-Warmth
    Beloved Authority Figure
    Guided and Independent Learning
    From Image to Lettering
    From Rhythm to Arithmetic
    Language—the Realm of Inner Images
    The Classroom Dialog
    Formative Education of the Whole Person through Art
    Individual and Community in the Artistic Process: In the Faculty
    Individual and Community in the Artistic Process: In the Classroom
    Practical Instruction
    Fostering Movement
    Individual Development and Developmental Divergences
    Fostering Rhythm throughout the School Year
    The Nine-Year-Old
    Summary

## Part 2

### Guidelines for the Education of the Child from 3–9
### An Outline of a
### Comprehensive Educational Approach

Foreword from the Original Edition . . . . . . . . . . . . . . . . . . . . . . . . . 73
    by Regina Hoeck and Sylvia Bardt

Goals of Education . . . . . . . . . . . . . . . . . . . . . . . . . . . . . . . . . . . . . . 75
    Respecting the Child's Individuality
    Accompanying the Child into Freedom and Response-ability
    Developing Social Competence
    Engendering All-Round Good Health
    Allowing Time for Lasting Development
    Holistic Education and Individual Support
    Overview of the Educational Process from Birth to Eighteen Years

Goals for Early Childhood Education . . . . . . . . . . . . . . . . . . . . . . . 78
    Educational Mandate Particular to the Kindergarten
    The Particular Goals and Approach for Kindergarten and Preschool
        Education
    Positive Learning Atmosphere and Reliable Relationships
    Adults as Role Models for the Children
    A Foundation for the Authenticity of Personality
    Engendering Coherence and Resilience
    Good Health through Education
    A Foundation for Lifelong Learning and Achievement
    Allowing the Time for Maturation
    Developmental Metamorphosis and Age-Appropriate Learning
    From Hand-Learning to Head-Learning
    Relaying Ethical and Social Values through Active Role Models

Continuation into Elementary School . . . . . . . . . . . . . . . . . . . . . . . 85
    School Is a Challenge
    Preconditions for Goal-oriented Learning
    Creating a Positive Atmosphere for Learning
    Preserving the Natural Joy of Life
    Developing and Strengthening Social Competency

Capacities Developed in Kindergarten. . . . . . . . . . . . . . . . . . . . . . . . . 91
   1. General Principles

   2. Free Play as an Activity that Fosters Development
        Forms of Play
        Building Ethical and Moral Values through Free Play
        Play Facilitation through Adults

   3. Movement, Physical Development, and Health
        Pedagogical Aspects
        The Motor and Physical Development of the Child
        Formation of Ethical and Moral Values through Movement
        Adult Support for Motor Development

   4. Speech Development
        Pedagogical Aspects
        Phases of Speech Development
        Fostering Ethical and Moral Values through Language
        Stimulation of Speech Development by the Adult

   5. Artistic Development through Rhythmic and Musical Education
        Pedagogical Aspects
        Cultivation of Music and Rhythm
        Formation of Ethical and Moral Values through Music
        Artistic Activities in Kindergarten

   6. Foundations of Mathematics and Science Education
        Pedagogical Aspects
        Laying the Foundation
        Formation of Ethical and Moral Values
        The Daily Kindergarten Routine

   7. Formation of Social Skills
        Pedagogical Aspects
        Developmental Steps towards Social Competency
        Formation of Ethical and Moral Values
        Fostering Social Competency

   8. Media Competency in Kindergarten and Elementary School
        Contact with Media
        Aspects of Developmental Psychology

Capacities Developed in the Elementary School................ 121
   9. Independence and Self-Reliance

   10. Fostering Health through Rhythm
       Rhythm in Class
       Structuring of Learning Steps

   11. Movement Education

   12. Speech, Reading Skills, and Foreign Languages

   13. Education through Art

   14. Introduction to Mathematics

   15. Ethical and Moral Values

The Education and Self-Education of the Educator............... 134
   1. Self-Education as the Foundation for Action
       Joy and Competency in Practical Work
       Artistic Competency

   2. Professional and Continuing Education

   3. Working Together
       Weekly Faculty Meeting and Child Study
       Working with Parents

   4. Cooperation between Kindergarten and Grade School

   5. Cooperation with Therapists, Doctors, and Expert Consultants

   6. Research and Quality Development
       Documenting the Development of the Children
       Research in Pedagogical Work
       Intention and Quality Standards

   7. Self-Governance
       Responsible and Entrepreneurial Attitude
       Managing the Organization
       Cooperation among Waldorf Institutions

   8. Integration into the Social Environment

   9. Architecture and Space Design

Bibliography ...................................................... 152

# From the Editor

## David Mitchell

The developmental stages of childhood provide the bedrock for Waldorf education. Observation and study of the child through these stages yield an understanding of the needs of children which is then transformed into a rich and diverse curriculum.

Translating these significant "signatures" into goals and standards set by state authorities has been a task of this book, thus the title *Developmental Signatures*. The research completed by colleagues in Germany that provided the material for this study on early childhood can be seen in parallel to the recent study in North America concerning Waldorf graduates. Published by the Research Institute of North America, the *Survey of Waldorf Graduates, Phase II* [1] strives to penetrate the results of the foundation set in the goals of this book. Together they should provide teachers, parents, and educators at all levels a window into this comprehensive education.

The photographs attempt to demonstrate visually what the text describes and provide a warmth that is a hallmark of this education. Of course no structure or set of abstract concepts can guarantee the success of an educational philosophy. Rather, it is the active, dedicated application by the Waldorf teachers, along with the mantle of warmth which exists in every Waldorf community, that makes the education filled with life.

Three phrases can best describe the cornerstones of Waldorf education: respect for the individuality within each child, love for the spirit of every child, and the transformation of the subject matter into living concepts by teachers who are also working on self-development. When these forces are in harmony,

---

1. Mitchell, David and Douglas Gerwin. *Survey of Waldorf Graduates, Phase II*, Wilton, NH: Research Institute for Waldorf Education, 2007. This study is available from Waldorf Publications, ISBN # 978-1-888365-82-5.

the Waldorf school is experienced, in its striving, as on a pathway leading to the ideals imagined by the founder.

It is our hope that this book will serve the schools as they explain their philosophy and also to help stimulate the greater educational debate in which we witness a constant attack on "childhood" and the disregard of developmental stages that are necessary to allow for the emergence of self-motivated, moral, and capable human beings.

# Foreword

## Susan Howard

We are very pleased to make this publication available to English-speaking readers in North America and throughout the world. This book contains the results of the first two parts of a three-part German study on the education and schooling of the young child. The first two parts are concerned with the child from ages three to nine in the context of education from birth to age eighteen; the third part of the project, currently underway, is exploring the education of the child from birth to age three.

Traditionally, "early childhood" has been defined as the period of development from birth through age eight, or, as it is often referred to in Waldorf education, the nine-year-change. However, the schooling of children in this developmental phase has not generally been approached as a continuum. Instead, it has been divided into preschool or nursery/kindergarten, and elementary school. In many countries these two realms have developed quite independently of one another. And in many cases, kindergarten and preschool education were seen as a phase of only general socialization and "child's play" and largely ignored by school and government authorities.

In recent years, however, brain research and other studies such as PISA (Program for International Student Assessment), conducted by the European Organization for Economic Cooperation and Development (OECD), have led to greater interest in the relationship between early (preschool) education and later development. A positive benefit has been the growing recognition of the importance of the formative early childhood years; more questionable outcomes have included political pressures for increased direct and explicit academic instruction at earlier ages, "outcomes-based" learning, and extensive testing and assessment for all children, even those of preschool age. In addition, school entrance age is being lowered by governments and educational authorities around the world to insure that national political and economic interests are well-served and that academic and technological instruction is "available" to all.

In this atmosphere of growing pressures, Waldorf educators throughout the world are increasingly challenged by governments and licensing authorities, parents and the public to articulate how, or whether, Waldorf education meets such externally-imposed curriculum goals. In Germany, where Waldorf education began and is now widely established, the nearly two hundred Waldorf schools and more than five hundred and fifty Waldorf kindergartens have been challenged to articulate their core values and practices in language that allows them to engage in productive dialogue with the authorities and the public.

The German Association (*Bund*) of Waldorf Schools, together with the International Association of Waldorf Kindergartens, formed a collaborative working group to explore and articulate how Waldorf education meets current expectations for educational standards and to attempt to expand the parameters of the wider educational debate. Comprised of kindergarten teachers, class teachers, researchers, and medical doctors, this collaborative working group chose to focus first on the educational needs of the developmental period of early childhood from age three to age nine, looking at the educational process as a continuum, beginning in nursery-kindergarten and extending through the lower grades to the nine-year-change, and then on into adolescence. A result of the first two phases of the study is the booklets called "Guidelines I and II," which we combine and publish here. The group is now in phase three, exploring the development and education of the child from birth to age three, in order to complete the picture of a comprehensive education of the child extending from birth to age eighteen.

The result of the working group's study is a comprehensive educational framework articulating the core values and practices of Waldorf education. At its center is the acknowledgment of the individuality of each developing child.

The kindergarten is seen as a place where children can acquire essential foundations for later life. Its curriculum includes free creative play, movement, language, sensory experiences, rhythmic-musical-artistic activities, a playful exploration of nature, and surroundings where adults are engaged in meaningful work processes. These elements provide a foundation for elementary school learning in such areas as mathematical-scientific thinking, literacy and linguistic capacity, artistic ability, and media competency. In addition, and perhaps ultimately more significant, is the development of qualities such as authenticity, independence, ethical values, social awareness, resilience, and health; these are the larger goals and "desired outcomes" of Waldorf education and form the basis for a fulfilling life.

The working group also explored the conditions required for successful schooling: what is needed for a healthy educational experience to take place. The group identified and described the following elements:

- The self-education of the teachers, engagement in a process of lifelong
professional development
- Close collaboration between teachers and parents
- Cooperation between the kindergarten and the elementary school
- Collaboration between teachers, doctors, therapists and specialists
- Colleagues engaged in research into the nature of their educational work and the learning of children
- Collegial self-administration with an entrepreneurial attitude, working together with other Waldorf schools
- Integration into the wider social and cultural community
- Attention to architecture and the shaping of the educational environment itself

The results of this working group's study in Germany are a great resource for reflection for deepening and renewing Waldorf and non-Waldorf educational practices both within the European community and throughout the world. As we strive to adapt in insightful and meaning-filled ways to meet the changing cultural climate in which our Waldorf schools and kindergartens find themselves, and to articulate both to ourselves and to others what it is that we stand for, this study by our colleagues in Europe can serve as a helpful stimulus and support.

This has been an enormous collaborative endeavor. In this spirit, this English language translation is a joint project of the Waldorf Early Childhood

Association of North America (WECAN), the Association of Waldorf Schools of North America (AWSNA), and the Research Institute for Waldorf Education. We are grateful to the Waldorf Curriculum Fund and the Waldorf Schools Fund for providing the necessary financial support and to AWSNA Publications for bringing it to print.

## Part 1

### Waldorf Education for Children Ages Three to Nine

# Introduction

In the present political situation regarding education with increasingly blurred boundaries between kindergarten and elementary school and younger mandatory school age dictated by lawmakers, it is imperative to take a closer look at the totality of child development. The principle of transformation is critical, the transformation of physical processes (growth, sensory-motor faculties, and so forth) into mental and spiritual faculties. Every step of this process takes time in order for these faculties to mature into long-lasting abilities. Education, whether in kindergarten or grade school, that is geared toward wholeness and sustainability must be founded on these stages of development.

The following overview sketches the guidelines for this kind of education. The different phases of development from ages three to ten will be illuminated from various perspectives in order to make it clear that this is a complex process. The individual stages of development build upon one another and may not be arbitrarily shortened or skipped without seriously endangering the physical and mental foundation for lifelong learning. Even though each child goes through the educational process quite individually, there are certain anthropological laws that apply. The health, creativity, and achievement potential of a young person depend upon the attention, or lack thereof, paid to these laws.

What is described here is only the outline of this educational process and in no way claims to be complete. We have met our goal if we have helped the reader understand the basic principles of Waldorf education.

This study was commissioned by the Bund der Freien Waldorfschulen and the International Association of Waldorf Kindergartens, and was conducted by a commission of physicians and educators including ourselves, Doerthe Baganz

(Berlin), Helmut Eller (Hamburg), Regina Hoeck (Überlingen), Thomas Jachmann (Villingen-Schwenningen), Margarete Kaiser (Dietzenbach), Kristin von Bleichert-Krueger (Leipzig), Helga Matthes (Berlin), Claudia McKeen (Stuttgart), Martyn Rawson (Stuttgart), and Almuth Voges (Kassel). Many colleagues from the elementary schools and kindergartens contributed to the final draft of this publication with their productive criticism and suggestions. We give you all our heartfelt gratitude!

– Dr. Rainer Patzlaff and
Dr. Wolfgang Sassmannshausen

# At the Center, the Individuality

**Steps on the Way to Human Freedom**

Commensurate with the view of human beings that Rudolf Steiner put at the center of his anthroposophical Spiritual Science, Waldorf education sees an inviolable individuality in every child. This individuality exists before conception and birth and, from its past, brings a very personal destiny with it into a present earthly existence, joined with still hidden impulses for the future that gradually emerge as a guiding theme or ideal in life, in the sense of Schiller's declaration, "Every individual person carries within himself, according to his disposition and purpose, a pure, ideal being, and the great task of his existence is to come into harmony with the unchangeable whole unity, in all its diversity, of that ideal."

The degree to which a person is successful in living and acting in harmony with his or her own "disposition and purpose," to that degree he or she is also free. It is the yearning for this freedom that connects all human beings. It is common to all and at the same time individual. It is the task of education to support and guide young people on their way towards this freedom.

**Education and Self-Education of the Child**

If one were to view the child as a mere object of teaching and conditioning, this would be the same as showing contempt for a person's individuality. In his early years, the child has the ability to "teach himself" (Schafer 2004). Further, he has the optimal prerequisites: an amazing, never-relenting drive to act and learn on the one hand, and on the other hand, limitless openness and the ability to devote himself to all impressions and influences from his

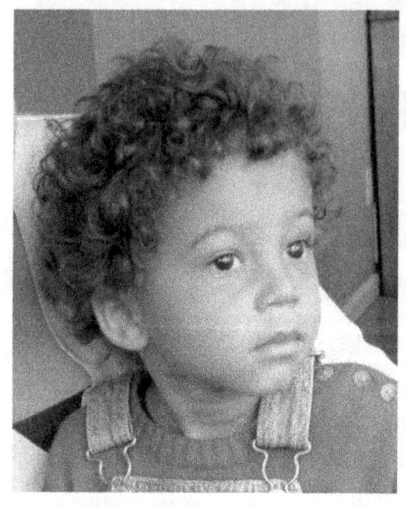

environment. Primal trust in the world and in his own capacities are what form the child's "startup capital."

But the ability for self-development is stymied when not met with a willingness of adults to responsibly provide for an appropriate environment in which the child shall grow up. Limited by instinct an animal's development is largely predetermined. In contrast a human being is born into the world as an unfinished, not yet defined being whose path is dependent on surrounding conditions. Therefore adults must create an environment conducive to development, an environment that offers stimulus for necessary experiences that encourage social interaction and is, at the same time, a protected environment wherein the child can develop unhampered.

The inseparable dual aspects of self-development and formation through the environment have been affirmed by modern research. Brain research has determined that human beings are the only living things who have the freedom to continually change their brain functions through their own exercise and learning processes (Eliot 2001, Huenther 2001, 2002). Social research has determined that freedom and autonomy of personality cannot develop in later life if the young child had no opportunity to firmly, securely bond with a caring adult during the first few years of life (Bowlby 1966, Ainsworth 1978). From the first moments of life, the child needs both education and self-education.

### The Physical, Vital and Mental Instruments of the "I"

Education in light of anthroposophy draws a distinction between the "I" as the unchangeable spiritual core of a human being and the three organizations that serve as instruments of the "I," allowing it to exist in the world and develop the individual's life themes. These three instruments are the physical organization, the vital force organization (that keeps the life processes going until death), and the mental organization.

The three organizations (or "members of the human organization," as Steiner called them) can serve only when the "I" has gained control over them and completely penetrated them so that they become the expression of the individuality. However, this is a lengthy process that requires careful tending throughout childhood and youth by parents, educators and, when necessary, by doctors and therapists, until the "I" has successfully penetrated these three instruments. When that time comes, we speak of the child's having reached his majority, and with it, formal education comes to an end. After that a person can only educate him- or herself and must take on the responsibility for realizing his or her own "disposition and purpose."

It is therefore the task of education to support the child in his efforts to anchor his individual "I" into the three organizations, or, to use an old expression, to incarnate, in order to fulfill that task. Adults need to have accurate knowledge of the developmental laws of the threefold organization and its complicated interactions in general. But they also need to sharpen their diagnostic gaze to be able to discern very individual problems present in different children. Wherever such problems occur, they are not to be evaluated as deficits of personality but rather as obstacles or challenges which the "I," as an integral spiritual being, meets on the way to complete integration into the threefold body.

**Salutogenesis as a Foundation for the Educational Process**

The interplay between the "I" and the threefold organization is not a routine occurrence in either children or adults. It is an extremely sensitive process prone to disruptions, requiring continual and renewed efforts to bring the whole organization into healthy balance. It is part of human freedom that these efforts can fail or be temporarily impaired. Herein lies the significant cause of illness.

Therefore, the goal of any true "art of education" must be to impart to the child the ability to meet the challenges of this process and master the obstacles. When this is successful, we speak of "health." By this we do not mean an absence of illness, but a possibility for the individual "I" to permeate the threefold organization in such a way that the full potential of the physical, mental and soul aspects can develop. Through this one gains the freedom to act according to one's own "disposition and purpose."

Health does not come about just by nature, so to speak. It requires certain conditions that need to be created and supported by education. In this, Waldorf education is in complete agreement with modern research. Investigations into salutogenesis (well-being and health) have resulted in the knowledge that health depends only in small measure upon biological factors and to an amazingly high degree upon certain mental/spiritual conditions that a person can or can learn to produce for him- or herself (Antonovsky 1993, 1997, Schueffel 1998, Grossarth-Maticek 1999). Specifically, this research into salutogenesis has identified three areas in which special conditions must be met for comprehensive good health.

The *physical-bodily organization* of the human being must gain the ability to deal with foreign substances coming from the outside so that they are either successfully transformed into bodily substances by the metabolic organs (as happens with food) or are successfully rejected by the immune system (as happens with a splinter or germs). This ability, as can be observed in infants and young children, can in no way be taken for granted. It has to be developed over time. Salutogenesis research has looked especially at the aspect of conflict and overcoming resistance, whereby the physical-bodily organization gains strength and the ability to assert its own form.

The *soul organization* is dependent on a strong experience of coherence, a secure feeling of connection with the world. This surely can come about only if the child has appropriate experiences that lead him or her to the absolute certainty that the world is a) principally transparent (understandable), b) manageable and pliant, and c) meaningful, so that also one's own efforts have meaning, and it is rewarding to try and meet the challenges of life.

The *spiritual organization* is strengthened to master problems through experiences of coherence. It is an unconditional requirement for developing courage and security in life. In wellness research this is usually referred to as "resilience" (Opp 1999). This means the individual can meet the hardships and adversities of life because he or she views them not as unchangeable facts, but as challenges that must be met. Resilience is rooted in the knowledge that one's own forces will grow in strength through conflict and that challenges provide opportunities for self-development.

Self-assertion of the physical body, coherence, and resilience together form the foundation that makes it possible for the individual to put into action his or her own very personal impulses and plans in life, thereby becoming productive and creative. This autonomy does not come about through intellectual learning processes but from active interaction with the world through direct experiences of all kinds, from achieving mastery of the physical body, from free, imaginative play, and from meeting life's challenges head-on. In short, self-education creates the foundation for health. Education that strives to provide the highest possible freedom for the individual to unfold his own strengths and abilities will therefore work in accord with the knowledge of salutogenesis down to every detail.

## Developing a Healthy Physical Organization

Various measures can be taken to strengthen the physical organization. The responsibility for these measures lies mainly with parents, but should also be acknowledged in kindergarten and elementary school. These include body hygiene, nutrition and food, exercise and a healthy environment without pollutants and high noise emissions. There are other factors important to the healthy growth of children, one of the most important being, for example, the aesthetics of the environment, which are perceived by the child very strongly, although entirely unconsciously. The architectural design of the classrooms, colors and pictures on the walls, the materials used, the way they feel and smell, the acoustics, and so forth, all affect the child clear down into his finer metabolic processes. The effects can be either strengthening or weakening (Rittelmeyer 1994, 2002).

The structure of time also has a profound effect on the child. Having a healthy rhythm to the days, weeks, months and years has an extraordinarily strong positive effect on a child's mental constitution and physical organization. The younger the child, the stronger the effect. (There is more on this theme later on.)

## Developing a Sense of Coherence through Direct Experience

First and foremost, the young child's task is to form and permeate his physical organization. The child dedicates himself, though unconsciously, to this task out of his own impulse with the greatest intensity and from the first moments of life. Nevertheless, the child would not accomplish this goal without caring adults because standing, walking, and speaking are not genetically programmed. Rather these abilities are gained through interactivity, through example and attention provided by adults. Accompanied and encouraged by caring adults, the child builds up his sensory faculties through practice, gradually gains mastery over his muscles used for movement, and thereby gains freedom to move around and get to know his environment. All of these efforts result in the building of differentiated neural networks in the brain, and these in turn form the basis for what later appears as imagination and cognitive thinking (Eliot 2001).

Of significance for self-development is having a lot of direct experiences when interacting with the world, that is, experiences gained with and through one's own body. The child must first be able to stand before he can understand the world. He must first grasp things physically before be can grasp them mentally. A child must smell things, taste, touch and handle them before he can experience the world as a manageable and transparent place. A feeling of coherence does not come about through intellectual comprehension but through hands-on

activities. These experiences in turn affect the structure of the brain and the development of motor and sensory skills, all contributing to the child's being able to make an increasingly stronger connection to his physical organization and his environment.

The lower senses (touch, movement, balance, well-being) play a special role which is not directed to the world outside, but to the inside, to one's own body. They signal one's position and movement in space (senses of movement and balance), coming into contact with things and conditions (sense of touch),

and perception of the internal organs as a whole (inner sense of well-being). Through movement in space, contacts through the skin, and the effect of gravity, the child experiences 1) his own body and 2) the spatial-material outside world in which the body exists. Here experience of the self and the world flow together.

Engendering a sense of coherence requires as many such dual experiences of self and the world as possible through the lower senses. And that is just what many children today are missing. Trust in one's own strength and the manageability of the world will not come about by talking to or cajoling the children. It happens by way of concrete, physical experiences through the senses. Cultivating the lower senses and movement are among the most urgent requirements in preschool, kindergarten and elementary education today. Complete development of sensory-motor skills is required to create the space for healthy soul and spiritual development. In this early phase, electronic media do nothing to promote development. They merely give the child the illusion of encountering the world and at the same time prevent any real encounters (Patzlaff 2004, Spitzer 2005).

**Development of Resilience**

What the child most urgently needs is a network into the immediate world, a social network of caring adults who set examples by their own behavior of what it means to stand in the world in such a way that one is not overwhelmed by the challenges of life. Through them the child learns to put events in perspective, master situations, be accepting and able to find meaning in events. Such experiences give the child a certainty that even those events that at first appear problematic can be put to rights. A positive attitude and joy in life are given their foundation, and these in turn give rise to the strength to meet today's challenges and grow from them.

A sense of coherence that is built upon resilience in this way promotes the motivation and ability for lifelong learning and development. A person who is accustomed to working through hindrances and opposition with courage, composure, a positive attitude and interest has the potential to realize his or her aims in life which he brought into this life from the world before birth. The basis for personal autonomy is not intellectual learning and conscious reflection but rather the feeling and willing forces that have been strengthened by coherence and resilience. Early childhood is the crucial phase for fostering these qualities. The unconscious immersion into a supportive and nurturing social and physical environment gives rise to the development of the personality and the emergence in freedom of the unique individual.

# Early Childhood Learning and Its Conditions

**The Special Nature of Early Childhood Learning**

Early childhood learning unfolds in a continually changing relationship to physical development. On the one hand it happens to and through the physical body, and on the other hand, the physical body is formed and structured through this learning. A young child opens himself up to all the influences and impressions of the environment with all of his senses. At the same time, the child cannot help but incorporate these experiences into a still pliable physical constitution. In a way, the world inscribes itself into the physical body. A familiar example of this is gaining the ability to speak. An infant's speech organs are such that any language in the world can be articulated. Over time, as the child actively acquires the mother tongue, he forms the tools for speech, all the way down to the anatomical structure, to meet the certain characteristics of that particular language. (The accent of a foreigner is a telltale sign of this phenomenon. And we are all familiar with the difficulties adults encounter in forming the sounds when trying to learn a new language.)

In contrast to the school-age phase, this phase of life is therefore an implicit, indirect process guided not by reflection and thought, but by activity and perception. All of the young child's mental activities are still completely directed to the outer world, connected through the senses with his environment. Many

facts prove that. A child's memory remains connected to his sensory surroundings (place memory) until well into the kindergarten years. For instance, often to the amazement of the adults at home, a child cannot say with whom he played during the day in kindergarten. But when he goes back to the kindergarten the next day and sees the toys he played with, then his memory is refreshed and he will continue the play activities as if there had been no interruption.

Another characteristic of the early years is that the motivation for play does not yet come from the outside but rather is determined by sensory impressions he has taken in at some point and now imitates in his play. During this time, the child does not live at a distance from things in such a way that would allow him to foster inner imagery or abstract (apart from sensory impressions) memory pictures. Only in the fifth or sixth year will the child begin to form such imagery and "organize" play with other children based on these memories and with certain rules that have been invented by the children.

**The Pedagogy of Creating an Environment: Order and Reliability**

To meet the special nature of early childhood learning in the best possible way, it is necessary to create surroundings that are rich in stimuli and possibilities for hands-on experiences. Learning that is connected to the physical body and its senses requires a differentiated environment that can be directly connected with the physical organs.

The child is confronted not only with the sensory, hands-on qualities of objects and materials, but also with a less obvious, but also important, factor, namely the order and reliability of the surroundings. As soon as children can walk, they begin to familiarize themselves with their environment, step by step. They begin with the rooms they live in, then the house, and finally with their surroundings as far as they are allowed. Full of curiosity and lively interest, they examine and investigate everything they see. Whatever they have come to know that is near their house is so important that they cannot wait to see it again on the next walk. They greet the things they have come to love like they were old acquaintances.

It is important for their life-sense that they see again today what they saw yesterday. Children in this age group feel compelled to make themselves at home in their environment as well as in their physical bodies. They want to put down roots. It is imperative that Mother and Father are still there on the next day and the day after, that the familiar things are still to be found in the same places, that everything is in its place. In that way they can deeply connect with their environment. If they continually experience this, then not only are their memory and spatial orientation capacities strengthened, but also their experience of coherence.

Children emphatically demand that they find ever again the order of things, thus signaling to adults how dependent they are on this experience. If those conditions exist, then the children can feel well and protected. If they do not exist, they the children can become restless and agitated. Any absence or disturbance of this order affects their feeling of well-being. A reliable order of things can give them security, much like a pilot who knows that the landing place awaits him when he returns after his exploratory flight.

## The Pedagogy of Creating an Environment: Rhythm and Repetition

What applies to the spatial surroundings goes also for the order and reliability of time. It has an extraordinarily positive, even healing, effect on children when their daily activities are not chaotic but rather rhythmically organized, following a certain order every day. Rituals play a large role here, especially during the transition times from day to night. In the morning rituals help the children to find their way from the unconsciousness of sleep into the daytime. In the evening a bedtime story,  a song, a prayer, or all three can help children to calm down for sleep after all the excitement of the day. Mealtime rhythms are also important, not only for reliability, but also for socializing and nutrition psychology.

In order to keep the daily rhythm from becoming mechanical, it should be embedded in weekly, monthly and yearly rhythms. Preschool-age children are not bored when events are repeated; to the contrary, they love the return of what they know and look forward to it. Festivals that are celebrated together become greatly anticipated high points of the year for the children.

The rhythmic structuring of time not only promotes mental balance,  but also benefits healthy sleep. The physical foundation is laid in early childhood for the undeveloped forces that later in adulthood will be called upon to deal with and master life situations that are not rhythmically ordered, in such ways that even in extreme cases of non-rhythmic schedules, adults can more or less maintain their health. Speaking in terms of salutogenesis, the feeling of coherence that is strengthened through rhythm and order bears fruit in adulthood in increased resources of resistance and resilience.

## Creating a Learning Environment: Facts and Connections

One of the conditions necessary for the experience of coherence is that the child comes to know that events and processes are connected, have

meaning, and serve a purpose. In earlier times children had plenty of opportunities for this experience in simply observing the daily activities of the surrounding adults: the farmer who planted, harvested and threshed the grain; the miller who ground it into flour; and the baker who made the flour into bread. Such perceptions, to name only one example, formed a sequence of actions

whose meaningful connection was directly apparent to the child's mind. From pure and simple observation, without any explanation, the child could see and experience what the activity of one person meant to another and how every activity related into a meaningful design of mutual effort.

In the technical environment of our day when so many processes are handled by machines, these relationships (even the activities themselves!) are invisible. Before, the mother had to first make a fire in order to cook a meal, but now she has only to open the refrigerator, put the food in the microwave, and take out hot food a few minutes later. How the kitchen machines function, what is necessary to manufacture them and make them work, where the food comes from, who prepares it—the child can

no longer see all of these efforts. There is no direct/visible correlation between the single activities and details for the child's consciousness, or any experience of coherence.

But children have a fundamental need to penetrate the world with understanding, to experience it as transparent, manageable and meaningfully structured. It is important for their development to have at least occasional experiences of what it means when, for example, after a meal the dirty dishes do not disappear into the dishwasher and reappear clean and shiny, but must be washed and dried by hand. Or when the heat that one needs for cooking is not turned on with a knob but instead must be made by piling up wood that has first been sawed and split, and then lighting it.

The point is not to send the children back to the Middle Ages, but to provide them with situations in which they can, through their own activity and observation, learn about processes that build upon each other in a meaningful way and have intrinsic connection. There is nothing better suited for this than the basic work activities in one's house and yard and in the practical crafts and professions as they were practiced as a matter of course in earlier times. By participating in such activities, and through repeating them in play, the child experiences coherence on a sensory basis, which precisely corresponds to the essential nature of his learning. The elementary school can build upon these kindergarten experiences by examining such themes in a more intellectual way.

## The Personality of the Teacher/Parent as a Formative Influence on the Child

We have discussed the significance of the pedagogical approach to creating an environment. This should not be taken to mean only the physical surroundings that can be perceived with the senses. To the child, the world is one. And part of that world is the inner thoughts and feelings of the adults. These inner realities are even more important for the child than the outer realities. A child can thrive under the poorest of outer circumstances if he is sure of his parents' love. And, conversely, the most beautiful toys mean nothing if the child lives in a loveless, even hate-filled, atmosphere.

Not every adult understands the undeniable certainty with which young children perceive the truth of the "inner realities" of adults. Whatever the adult does or says, children sense the moral quality behind it. Gesture, facial expression, nuance of voice, and the look in one's eyes all tell the child a lot more than is often acknowledged. Judgments and thoughts, emotions and intentions of adults have a tremendous impact on the young child, even if they are not verbalized. A child is not able to dryly observe from a distance as an adult can. A child is existentially at the mercy of all impressions, positive and negative. Their effects penetrate down into even the subtle structures of the physical, vital and mental organizations. For this reason, the environment

of thoughts, feelings, intentions and desires of adults is of great significance to the child. It can promote or hinder the child's development.

What adults have caused can seriously impact the destiny of a child. It does not even have to be negative thoughts around the child; it is enough when the adults' words and deeds are continually clashing, when the "inner realities" are not aligned with the outer expression, when the adult is no longer in harmony with his or her own self. Such behavior goes against the nature of young children, who are always at one with their behavior and have the unspoken expectation that others are also "true" in this respect. With complete abandon, and no calculated distance, children throw themselves into their environment at every moment and identify with it, even when the impressions are of a burdensome nature. Children live in the unity of the world and the "I," of the inside and the outside, and they are dependent upon meeting people who are likewise authentic and in harmony with themselves. The extent to which the child can have these meetings determines the foundation for mental health and, with it, the basis for later conscious striving for the identity and authenticity of his own adult personality.

**Self-Education of the Educators**

One can see what a responsibility the educating adults carry. Their personalities are the real formative environment for the child and have a greater effect than any educational program, however well-intentioned. Whenever the child experiences authentic personality, the foundation is laid for a deep, secure feeling of coherence between the inner and outer worlds.

Children naturally want to follow, with unconditional trust, the examples of adults. Their imitation does not stop with actions. There is also joyful immersion into the qualities and values of adults. Interest in the world, joy in life, moral integrity, and so forth, have value not only for the adults who cultivate them, but especially for the child who experiences them. A person's resilience in later life is dependent on the development of such inner values and qualities. They are cornerstones in situations when one has to weather life's worst storms, and they give meaning to one's own life, a meaning that is not only conceptual but also gives strength.

Children live towards this goal. That is why it is not so important for a child what adults know but rather who they are and what they do. There is an expectation that adults can live up to only if they work on themselves. "Education is first and foremost self-education of the educator." More than all other factors it is the personality of the adult which becomes the "formative" influence on the child.

## The Significance of Free Play

As social research has found, one who is fortunate enough to experience a solid, intense connection with a caring adult from earliest childhood is well-equipped to mature in later life into a truly free, self-determining personality (Bowlby 1966, Ainsworth 1978, Spangler 1996). The same impact goes for the pedagogical structuring of the child's environment: if it is reliably ordered and rhythmically structured, emotionally grounded on a soul level, and mentally authentic, then the child has something to hold onto. This dependability allows the child to unfold in a completely different activity, namely, in free play. Here the children are on their own and not under any outer authority or preconceived purpose or instruction. They follow only their own impulses. The themes and content of play are created from within. In principle, free play does not require any encouragement, or at least no directions, from adults.

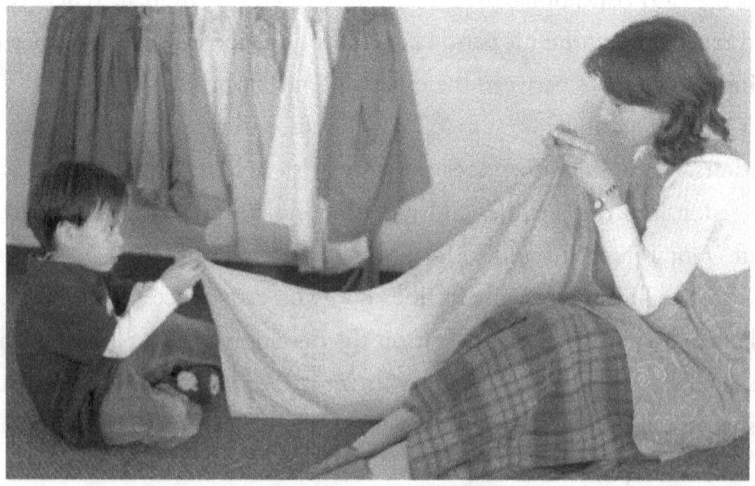

At the beginning of its development, an infant playfully investigates its own body. It practices eye-hand coordination and motor skills gradually. As soon as an infant can purposely take hold of something, it devotedly busies itself with all the things that it finds in its surroundings and  investigates each object with all it senses before going on to the next object. When the child can move freely about the room and observes the many daily activities of adults, then play takes on a different, more imaginative character. The child will make a toy out of the most unlikely object, for the child has assigned a "meaning" to the object that can change again in the next moment. For instance, a piece of wood can serve as an iron, then a trumpet, then a piano, and so forth.

This is the time when adults like to give toys to children. But if the toy is a true-to-life representation of some useful object in every detail, then the child's spontaneity and imagination are unnecessarily curtailed, and the child will quickly lose interest. Objects that are free from fixed purpose are much more suitable as toys. Materials from nature such as pine cones, chestnuts, rocks, roots, branches, large and small pieces of wood, and also pieces of cloth, buckets and tubs, empty boxes and boards offer the child a practically inexhaustible field of activity in which to unfold his or her creative potential. Here it is the child's assigning the meaning to the object that is the crucial factor. The activity sparked from within transforms into imagination and thinking and forms the foundation for learning in school.

During free play the child unconsciously internalizes his or her experience of the world. As an example: the child can literally "grasp" the natural laws when, for instance, he builds a tower from some unformed natural materials. He can experience all the laws of mechanics within the activity, and we can observe how the child, when left to his own, carries on with his "self-education." This happens through active connection with the world and not through intellectual observation and reflection. This has nothing to do with scientific research as yet, but rather with the most intensive perception of the phenomena. This is the best preparation possible for the study of the natural sciences in later schooling and natural science research in later life.

# The Transition to Elementary School Learning: When Is the Right Time?

**Play and Social Behavior of the Six-Year-Old**

Four-year-old children generally find the theme for their play activities spontaneously, born in the moment, prompted by an activity or an object they encounter in their romp through the apartment or through the kindergarten. Six-year-olds, in contrast, do not necessarily require such prompting from the outside, but they can develop their play idea based on a memory of a previous experience. They try to recreate what they saw or experienced at a previous time. In this activity they prove to be most determined and persistent, as when they, for example, comb through all the rooms of their home to collect all suitable furnishings for making a railway train and gather together everything that seems useful to them for that task. There is also a great difference in how they proceed from here, in comparison to younger children. A four-year-old is already satisfied when a few chairs are arranged in a row—one behind the other—making a train car and "riding" in it for a while. Six-year-old children, however, will set great store in providing the train with all the details they can remember, and they will also reenact the railroad journey as realistically as possible.

Moreover, it is important for them that they play together with other children, mostly the same age, and governed by rules and rank which they determine themselves. While they may like it when younger children join in, the six-year-olds are the ones who direct the play and assign roles to the younger children.

Here we see a new stage in the development of the child. The six-year-old can form an exact notion of how his play idea should be actualized because he can set a goal for himself, independent from outer promptings. A new faculty is

emerging which will, in later years, become very important: the faculty to form a precise mental image of a future course of action, in other words, anticipation. The six-year-old already commands a respectable amount of overview capabilities and uses them to organize his play into meaningful action sequences. On the other hand he is still child enough to spontaneously integrate new elements that emerge during play and flexible enough to incorporate them into the play process.

The awakening of social competency counts among the striking attributes of six-year-old children in kindergarten. They like to take the initiative in free play, for example, involve the younger children, show them how to do it right, and volunteer for tasks like setting the table. They are enthusiastic if they are given the privilege of substituting for the kindergarten helper if she should be out. They are the knowledgeable ones among the kindergarten crowd, the "kings and queens," and they delight in being recognized as such.

Experience teaches that this status can hardly be achieved before the sixth or seventh year, not least because only now the motor skills have been developed sufficiently to be able to fulfill tasks independently. It also takes children between two and three years to gain experience in their kindergarten before they can direct the younger children with circumspection and prudence. These successes foster their self-esteem, generating a developmental surge that strengthens their ability to meet the challenges in elementary school. Often we can observe how especially the boys gain from being granted the benefit of increased status in their last year of kindergarten.

Today more and more children can gain little experience in relating naturally with younger or older siblings at home because they are the only child. For them, the mixed-age kindergarten group is like an "extended family" that offers them important practical experiences which culminate in being allowed to help a younger child from the position of being the older one, to be responsible for the younger one. The homogeneous age group of the grade school class does not offer this opportunity. Children sent to grade school too early will miss this experience. The presumed "loss" of time is more than compensated for by the strength the child gains in the last kindergarten year for his further development. This does not preclude any special circumstances which may lead to a different decision, but allowing the young child to reap the fruits of his or her kindergarten time in tranquility is an essential consideration.

## Intellectual Precocity and Dissociation

Linking the beginning of elementary school to a child's chronological age is a longstanding tradition and today is more and more put to question. "School maturity" is a developmental stage that is expected to occur around the sixth birthday, or the seventh year of life. However, in times past, a specific assessment by a school physician was performed to ascertain if the six-year-old was truly mature enough to begin elementary school, which sometimes resulted in postponement of the start of school for that child. Physical criteria were of importance, such as the change of teeth or maturity of appearance and motor and sensory development.

Such assessments are no part of the decision when, of late, laws are passed that set the time for starting school earlier and earlier, giving parents the possibility to enroll their children in grade school when they are only three or four years old. This trend is supported by the opinion, borne in business circles and often adopted by politicians, that the intellectual potential of today's children is lying idle for

too long in kindergarten and should be fostered and challenged much earlier in order to prepare the children in a timely manner for the challenges of their later work lives (careers). If we follow this line of reasoning, the child's "school maturity" would indeed occur many years earlier than so far assumed. In some of today's children we can indeed observe a remarkable intellectual awareness and achievement readiness before they reach the traditional age for starting school. But if we examine such children more closely, we find quite frequently an acute discrepancy, gaps between the various levels of their development. Perhaps they are in one way, intellectually, ready for school, but that is not at all true in regard to their physical, soul and social development. We can also find other forms of dissociation, such as when intellectual development is not in step with physical maturity, and so forth. In each case, such dissociation can be seen as a sign of a lack of stability in the foundations of development, which would not be able to meet the manifold challenges of school in the long run.

We need to take the long-range perspective into account. We should not be hoodwinked by the early successes of a child in the first grades. We generally cannot see the true elasticity and resilience of the foundations in body and soul, which are built in childhood, until the upper classes are reached—where the soul's resilience will be challenged to a much greater degree to deal with the inevitable crises. The scientific studies we have available to date document that children who start school too early show a conspicuous setback in the higher grades, and often have to repeat one or more classes (Beilenberg 1999), which then has the additional effect of weakening their self esteem.

Taking intellectual precocity as a benchmark for the start of academic learning is to disregard the requirements for healthy development as outlined above. The young human being needs a full measure of coherence and resilience for mastering his later life-tasks; to develop such resilience and coherence, he must be afforded sufficient opportunity for permeating the organization of body and soul with his individuality and shaping them into a full-fledged instrument for his personality. The cognitive and intellectual capacities can only unfold in a healthy manner when they go hand in hand with creativity and social competency—not at their expense.

But for that, the child needs time. In Waldorf education we strive to give the children this time, to base school readiness not on mindless philanthropic impulses but motivated by a therapeutic challenge. We must make sure that the developmental foundations which they need in order be able to live in accordance with their own "nature and purpose" are not compromised by pulling the rug out from under the children's individuality.

## The Seven-Year Rhythm—A Health-Generating Principle

The problem of dissociation is not limited to preschool times. We observe a widening chasm in the various levels of development also during their school years, manifested particularly by an earlier onset of puberty. At that time the development of the physical body forms in glaring contrast to the child's soul-life, which still appears childlike. This phenomenon differs from precocious intellectual faculties which are ahead of sensori-motor and social development in the preschool years; the problems in puberty are created by the unsupported one-sided acceleration of physical maturity.

It is not productive to simply deplore such phenomena. They are expressions of the overall acceleration which characterizes our modern, hectic lifestyle. But how do we meet this enormous challenge of our future? The wider the gaps between developmental processes, the more urgently we must act pedagogically, to even them out and harmonize them in the interest of the healthy development of our children.

In Waldorf education an awareness of the seven-year rhythm affords us the opportunity to employ such harmonizing and compensating pedagogy. We can therapeutically adjust to meet the developmental processes appropriately. It is often assumed that we are dealing with a natural rhythm that occurs by itself, following the same laws as many other biological rhythms in our organism. But this is not the case. The seven-year rhythm is not set by nature, just like the year is not "naturally" divided into seven-day weeks. However, we are not dealing just with mystical number games. No, the seven-year rhythm has salutogenic relevance when it is considered as a developmental gauge in pedagogy. This rhythm marks a timeframe, like a benchmark, which is necessary to help stabilize the complex structures in a young person's physical, soul and mental/spiritual organization on a certain stage of development by either gently slowing down a too-rapid advancement or aggressively nurturing those processes that are developing too slowly. If allowed to align with this health-generating rhythm, the child receives a strong foundation for its entire life (Hildebrandt 1998, Schad 2004).

An education that allows young children and youths to take their time from one seven-year period to the next has beneficial effects, as pedagogical practice shows. An artistically-inspired approach to education helps the children overcome the problem of dissociation as it brings all faculties of body and soul into balance. Under such guidance, slower-maturing faculties come to blossom, which would never have unfolded under the pressures of a school system focused on achievement and accelerated learning. If we understand the seven-year rhythm within this paradigm as a pedagogic-therapeutic benchmark to strive for, it takes on an important role in fostering health in a time when developmental problems in childhood are increasing.

## The Metamorphosis of the Forces Shaping the Body

One of Rudolf Steiner's most profound discoveries was the concept that the forces needed by the young child in his first phase of development for building and structuring his physical organization are the same forces that help him in the second phase in building the forces for the powers of imagination and memory (Steiner 1907, 1921, 1922, Kranich 1999). During the first phase, the child unconsciously works on schooling his sensory faculties and mastering his musculature by developing both his gross- and fine-motor skills. His inner organs unfold into full functioning, and ever more complex neuron processes are created in the brain. Generally after about seven years, a first stage of maturity is reached in the physical development, and part of the building forces and faculties are by nature no longer needed for growing and building the inner organs. This part does not just disappear, but is fully available for other tasks, for example, to grow and support the powers of the soul and mind in developing the imaginative faculties, memory and the ability for academic learning.

Steiner pointed to the consequences that occur when these forces are prematurely harnessed to academic learning. When they are diverted from the uncompleted task of building the physical structure, then the hampering of a healthy, resistant physical constitution may result, even if at first very subtle, almost imperceptible. While comprehensive empirical proof is still pending, numerous experiences in practical education appear to validate this hypothesis. Meanwhile scientific long-term studies have not been able to prove conclusively any lasting advantages that very early enrollment brings for young children. On the contrary, the probability of having to repeat a class is significantly higher for this group than for children who enter school at the traditional point in time (Bellenberg 1999).

Therefore it is of utmost importance for optimum health and achievement in later life to wait with beginning school-learning until the forces building the physical body are fully transformed into the forces that develop the imagination and until the learning process can be released from its earlier ties directly to the senses. Whenever we force a developmental stage (in this case, by too early a start of academic learning), there is a danger that we interrupt the

comprehensive, differentiated maturation process of the physical organization and thus potentially weaken the foundation of the child's health.

Every adult can validate, from the personal experience of being weakened by fever, the close connection between forces building the physical organism and those building the imagination. During such a time the body needs all vital forces to maintain its life functions and to regain health, and it is more difficult to have concentrated, focused images and thoughts.

## The Launch of the Faculty of Imagination

The physician can determine from a variety of physical symptoms when the imaginative faculty is ready for development (change of teeth, shape, mature sensori-motor skills, and so forth). But he can see only the outer aspect of the phenomenon. On an inner level, the release of these powers is connected to a profound change of soul life. The child steps out from the confinement of the senses and now gains command of independent soul faculties, which he employs consciously on the inner planes.

The earlier stage is well illustrated in this example: a four-year-old who, on hearing the word *S-Bahn*, inquired what the people in this tram were eating. [*S-Bahn*, meaning "tramway" is pronounced "Ess-Bahn," and *ess* in German means "eat"!—trans.] In contrast to imagining things in a concrete, literal way, the child who is ready to enter school commands a faculty of imagination that functions independently of concrete sensory impressions. Memory too grows free from the link to physical, concrete presence of place (local memory, as in the example above) and becomes autonomous. It can happen that a child of that age is surprised to discover that she can visualize a person who is far away in full detail and whenever she wishes to do so. Memory becomes available, independent of presence in space and time; inner images can be formed and now spark thinking processes, just as they were previously sparked by sensory perceptions.

An experiment conducted by Swiss psychologist Jean Piaget illustrates this transition. Two identical glass vessels were filled each with the same amount of water in the presence of four- to five-year-olds. When questioned, the children found the amounts of water in A and B to be the same. Then, in full view, a third vessel C, this vessel being much taller and narrower than the other two, was filled with the same amount of water. When asked again, most of the children thought that there was more water in vessel C because the water level was higher, and some thought there was less water in vessel C because it was narrower. Children who were ready to enter school, however, stated correctly that the amounts in all three vessels were the same (Piaget 1973).

This experiment is not undisputed because it could lead to the false conclusion that younger children are stupid. Actually they are in no way stupid; they just experience the world differently based on the object-oriented intensity of their perceptions. The experiment points to an important fact: What we see here is not a quantitative transition from a less bright to a bright child. No, it is a qualitative leap that brings with it a transformation of the child's overall relationship to perception.

The younger children are still guided by outer sense impressions and answer based on an object's visually prominent attributes (width and height), whereas the older children use as a resource their memory-image, which tells them that the amount of water stayed unchanged by pouring it into different vessels. They can evaluate and conclude that the amount must be the same, in spite of the taller water column or the narrowness of the vessel. Their freed forces, powers of memory and imagination

are available to them for the mental processing of perception beyond the visual image.

Only when this transformation has occurred should the child be exposed to academic learning in school. As outlined above, it is only now that the child can safely employ the formative powers which were formerly needed to build the body structure. Only now he can use these powers to form inner images and thoughts without jeopardizing his healthy physical development. Often the children themselves discover this new faculty of dealing with inner images when they begin to take great pleasure in solving poetic puzzles which challenge their vivid powers of imagination.

# The First School Year

**From Implicit to Explicit Learning**

When the child is ready to enter school, her behavior and needs change radically in regard to learning. Before this phase, the child was fully immersed in imitating her surroundings. The mother, for example, inspired the child to imitate her own vacuum cleaning and in turn the child used a suitable stick and matching sounds for her "vacuum cleaning" activities. The meaning and purpose of certain movements were not moderated by thought processes but were derived directly from actively joining in the activity. Her learning was an implicit process. But now that is no longer enough. The child yearns for explicit learning, for having a teacher guide her through methodically sequenced learning and practice processes that require active effort. She has direct questions and wants to know about reasons and interconnections.

However, this transformation does not happen all at once. In healthy development the imitation faculty extends into the early school years, and the

teacher can make use of it, as the children initially learn many things easily by imitation, playing a recorder, for example, or moving through a room in a specific pattern, speaking a poem in a foreign language, performing a rhythmic-musical exercise, and so forth. And yet, this situation is widely different from learning in early childhood because these are now directed processes, guided by the teacher. Children who are ready to begin school have a deep need for such guided processes, which we call classroom instruction. Their orientation is still intensely focused on the model of the teacher, but at the same time they consciously make the effort of repeating and correcting in order to improve their faculties. They are taking ownership of their learning process.

The burning eagerness many children show in this process offers rich opportunities to the teacher for leisurely (without pressure or achievement stress) allowing a gradual post-maturation process for things that need particular nurturing nowadays: first of all, the language faculty, but also motor skills, body and spatial senses, the memory capacity, the ability to concentrate, and so forth.

These teacher-guided activities must not disintegrate into mechanical drill practice. It is important that the teacher strive for artistic ways of conducting the lessons and for responding sensitively to the abilities of each child. If successful, she is not the feared but the beloved authority, which the children emulate in order to become like her in knowledge and skills. Such a teacher will find that the children heed meaningful rules and take daily delight in having order, reliability and clarity in the classroom, brought about through the beneficial influence of the teacher. They feel empowered down to bodily well being, and their development is supported by this influence.

## Learning in an Atmosphere of Soul-Warmth

When we talk about the forces that build the body transforming into forces of learning and memory that are now available to the child, we could give rise to the misunderstanding that the time has come to address the child intellectually like an adolescent or an adult. That does occur frequently today, and experience shows how damaging such one-sidedness can prove to be. The child needs a long transitional period in order to complete the shift from the outer-oriented young child that is ruled by the senses to becoming an inner-oriented, reflective youth. During this transitional time, the child's way of learning is still completely enveloped in a soul energy and strongly appeals to the child's sensitivity.

The experience of coherence, which is fundamental to overall healthy development, once more becomes the central theme of education. While the young child experienced this coherence through physical activity and imitation, it must now be attended to on the soul level for the school-age child.

Brain researchers like Manfred Spitzer point out emphatically that the child will gain free, creative access to the subject matter he learns in school only if this learning happens in an emotionally positive atmosphere. Scientific research shows that no true learning takes place unless there is a warm relationship on a soul level between teacher and student, and without this relationship, it is only an intellectual, mnemonic drill leading to mechanically "crammed" knowledge (Spitzer 2002).

A positive class atmosphere is only the cornerstone. Not to be confused with *Gemütlichkeit* (coziness) or chummy ingratiation, what really counts here is to avoid a one-sided development of the thinking faculties of the child leading him towards a kind of impersonality and even mechanicalness. On the contrary, we want to keep the thinking powers as long as possible in touch with the powers of sense perception. All children at this age level naturally take in things from their surroundings; they do not yet have the motivation to set themselves apart from the environment as older children characteristically can do.

## Beloved Authority Figure

The children not only need but also seek out a learning environment that offers a positive class atmosphere. This finds clear expression in their adoration of the classroom teacher; they seek her personal affection and long for her acknowledgment. Another indication of this is the frequent observation that the children will do their homework less for their own sakes, but more and especially for the teacher's sake, whose reaction they anticipate with excitement. This may continue for several years if the teacher is indeed beloved. No teacher can elevate herself into having authority over the students. The students themselves are the ones who make her into an authority by giving her the gift of their respect and affection. A teacher can win this gift only by meeting the students with a rich measure of interest, openness and enthusiasm. Students want to be seen, want to be understood; for that, a teacher needs to offer more than a well-structured way of teaching—human qualities are in demand here.

But the teacher must also offer didactic skill and in-depth knowledge of the material so that she can guide them towards gaining new skills or entering new fields of knowledge. Indeed, students will trust the guidance of a person when they recognize her as a "master teacher."

A teacher's authority, if understood correctly, does not manifest as a challenge that the students have to live up to. Rather, such authority emerges when teachers work on themselves and strive to meet the challenges in their own personal development. This striving safeguards them from routine and indifference. A positive learning atmosphere can spring up in their classes.

**Guided and Independent Learning**

Well-understood authority does not mean that a teacher has an exclusive lead role in class. Rather, the respect for the individuality of a child demands a sufficient measure of trust in his own faculties and space for their development. A well-conducted class will shuttle in a healthy way between phases of guided and independent learning.

Such learning situations are conducive to the development of individuality and are especially needed in today's world because students enter school with diverse levels of readiness. Some have been coached how to write, read and do calculations; some have learned all on their own; others are still far away from being able to handle such tasks and are in need of sensitive guidance. The general trend toward ever-stronger individualization further adds to this heterogeneity in children who start school. Many children display early on very individualized traits, coupled with radical originality, authenticity and creativity, and consequently demand individual attention from the teacher. That is the only way the teacher can become a "beloved authority" for them, someone whom they can eagerly emulate in the first years of school.

The students can develop a profound yearning for an independent mode of learning that allows them to discover and explore their own dormant powers. This yearning in its highest and purest form leads to a passion for learning and taking joy in the activity. This type of learning can manifest in multiple ways in artistic and practical classes. Moreover, already in the first grade, small project groups can work together independently, with only the aid and advice of the teacher. For example, all students can freely cooperate in a painting assignment, whose theme they have chosen themselves. Or they can perform a little theater play that emerged while they played by themselves. In the upper grades, the students can make self-directed choices about thematic projects in social, environmental and nature studies and work on them jointly. In school, abilities such as reading, writing and arithmetic are usually taught as individual classes of their own, but here they can find practical application. We also should not underestimate the fact that we can strengthen the ability to practice through such self-directed activities without diminishing the motivation to learn.

**From Image to Lettering**

The further development of the child relies to a strong degree on the teacher's ability to guide the child's transition from working with the hands to working with the mind, from learning through the limbs to learning through the powers of memory, imagination and thinking. If guided in the right way, the child will not feel a one-sided emphasis on intellectual faculties, but will feel approached also through the feeling and willing sides of his being, on which the thinking powers can build.

Let us look at the introduction of letters in order to illustrate how Waldorf education seeks to put this principle into practice, down into the methodology of our classes. In the first grade the child is not only faced with a "sign," he is not asked to just memorize this sign matched with its phonetic meaning; rather, the teacher first tells a story, into which the child plunges with all his imagination and fantasy, even if he can already read.

Next follows a blackboard sketch of one situation from the story, which the children draw into their own books and, with a few bold strokes of chalk, a letter emerges from within the picture on the blackboard. From there, the letter is drawn apart from the picture, albeit abstractly, but now the children have a soulful connection with this shape, which otherwise would have stayed alien to them, and they experience inner coherence. They follow the transition from image to letter with active understanding, they create it actively with their own hands, and they are able to apply it and experience the meaning embedded in this process. Incidentally, this way of proceeding corresponds to the development of writing in the history of mankind, whereby sensorial-concrete pictures turned step-by-step into abstract symbols.

Many people object by saying that the image-oriented introduction of writing is obsolete for children who can already read and write before they start school. But they overlook that children who learn, for example, from their older siblings how to read and write, are simply imitating them, while the child who is truly ready for school not only wants to perform, but also longs to understand the material inside and out. The method described herein gives them this opportunity by addressing not only the cognitive faculties, but also the feeling and willing powers. This method ensures that the whole person can participate in the introduction of the letters and before the activity of writing becomes mechanical.

**From Rhythm to Arithmetic**

When introducing the realm of numbers, Waldorf education seeks to involve the whole person. The students are acquainted with numbers and later multiplication tables not only through simply naming the numbers or writing down the corresponding symbols, but through rhythmical movement sequences. The succession of numbers is practiced every day and memorized in ever-new variations through hand clapping, jumping and running.

The path to multiplication begins when the children count out loud in unison and accent each second or third number by either agreeing to *not* clap or to *only* clap or to count that number without saying it out loud. This makes high demands on the children's awareness and their mind-hand coordination. The child can thus master the multiplication tables through physical, sensori-motor activity and prepare the ground for purely abstract calculations later. Mathematics is "saved" from turning into a dead, incomprehensible foreign body in the soul experience of the child. Rather, this path offers a profound, nearly instinctive experience of coherence. Multiplication is embedded in one's own activity, it is recognized as a higher level of counting, and the child grasps the meaningful connection between the world of numbers and practical activities in daily life (Schuberth 2001).

This way of teaching elicits mathematical understanding from within the body, where it is indeed rooted, as illustrated by the wondrous numeric proportions of the various bones and the rhythmic organization of pulse and breath. The structure-forming laws that are at work in the body on an unconscious level now extend, like a reflection of light, into the rhythmic learning activities of the child, steered by will and conscious coordination. Later, in the science classes, this activity will be raised fully into the light of consciousness.

The child's attitude towards the work is very profoundly impacted by the way we guide him into this process. It is important that the fundamental classes in the four arithmetic disciplines proceed from the whole to the parts, rather than as conventionally done the other way around, from the part to the whole. In Waldorf education we generally start from the sum when introducing addition, from the product in multiplication, and so forth, because the child has a concrete experience of things and associates number with practical realities. There is indeed a difference if we start from the whole, which then splits into parts, or if we view the world as simply an agglomeration of fragments which line up in a purely additive manner. We will later also see a great difference in the social and environmental stance of the persons who have formed a holistic view of the world shared by all human beings, instead of just thinking of their own property.

### Language—the Realm of Inner Images

Children love stories and fairy tales, fables and legends, and it is important for a teacher to realize why children have such a hunger for them. These tales contain a lot of wisdom and life experience, profundity and cleverness, thoughts and logic, expressed not in abstract terms, but in images. These stories delight the soul by painting entire landscapes and countless details that match the sensorially perceived world in color and immediacy, but it is the child herself creating this in her own fantasy; in other words, the pictures are her own accomplishments. Between the young child's hands-on, sensory grasp of the world and the adolescent's or adult's mental, thinking comprehension of the world stands the pictorial, imaginative way of understanding the world, which always constitutes a creative act.

Language is the key medium for unfolding the imaginative world in children. Language has the power of translating everything the storyteller sees with her inner eyes into the children's own inner vision. The more the storyteller can vividly experience the imaginative expanses in herself and put them into words—freely or by reading out loud—the more colorful and formative will be the imaginative powers of the children. This effect is at its most powerful when the teacher acquires the ability to vibrantly and dramatically tell a story from memory. Also, the reading of a suitable, artistically rendered story can be very effective if it proceeds with vivid participation.

The children are nourished by such experiences, and they want them every day. They are not driven by a need for information or knowledge, but by the yearning for intuitive exploration of the rich inner worlds, which are opening up to them symbolically and imaginatively through the medium of language. Even though our time is flooded with technical images, there is no decrease in the hunger for such experiences. To the contrary, it grows in the same measure as the children feel increasingly emotionally disconnected from their environment. School here fulfills an essential cultural task, yes, and a cultural mandate—less intellectually than developmentally—to foster the ability for empathy, differentiation and imagination as well as social sensitivity.

It is essential that the subject matter of the story be appropriate for each age level. In a Waldorf school, the children are exposed in the first three grades to fairy tales and myths, proceeding then to fables, legends and sagas, and finally they hear the stories of the Old Testament as part of an introductory world- and cultural-history class. In this process, they can follow the path of humankind, mirroring their own evolutionary path in a certain sense. At the same time the educator deeply influences the ethical-moral development of the child through the choice and dramatization of his verbal images and stories, provided he avoids sermonizing and allows the images to fully speak for themselves.

**The Classroom Dialog**

Many childhood experiences can be truly understood and processed only after the child has had the opportunity to talk about them in a good conversation. In such dialog, a relational space is created in which experiences can be exchanged, knowledge transmitted, appointments made, conflicts verbalized and solved.

Here we can also practice the faculty of good and precise listening. Such social conversation spaces can no longer be taken for granted in our times—we have to make an effort to first establish them again. Therefore it is an important task of the school to establish and maintain a culture of verbal dialogue, particularly in the first grades. It is the foundation for all instruction in class.

**Formative Education of the Whole Person through Art**

We normally associate kindergarten with playing and grade school with learning. But there is not such an abrupt cut between the two phases of child development. The faculty for playing is still a precious gift, which we must foster also in the first grades of school. In a certain sense, this gift is a primordial cultural technique for developing initiative, devotion and interest, joy of discovery and mental creativity, the ability for teamwork and social competence. But it is in particular this creative, formative process that often develops too slowly or incompletely in more and more children today because they do not receive the corresponding inspiration. Television, video games, computers and iPods are paralyzing this process more than fostering it, even though the advertisements allege the opposite. Waldorf education therefore consciously nurtures a fantasy-rich learning style through play, art and practical activities, not only in the subjects offered but also in the methodology of teaching, Painting and drawing, making music and performing theater plays are activities that fully answer the children's needs for an active connection with the world. And at the same time they stimulate a guided process of learning and practicing which has a formative effect on the whole person. The teaching style emerges freely from the children's joy in shared activities and their enthusiasm for the audible or visible work of art, not from a rigid system of rules.

If we are able to bring that about, the success motivates everyone—students and teachers—to reach even further, and the children expand their capabilities as a result of their own, inner drive. A refined culture of feeling and perception is rooted in this process, enhancing the joyful initiative, independence and social competency that we wish to see in later years in an adult who is open to the world and humanity. The capacity for empathy and socially creative fantasy, the will to create and openness towards the new—these qualities are commonly listed as the key faculties on which our future depends. These faculties have no chance to form if the intellectual and mental faculties of the child are prematurely displaced from their natural connection with the forces of willing and feeling through an education with a one-sided emphasis on the intellect, pervasively relying on abstract terms, definitions, and processes. A child who has developed in a healthy way will, even after reaching school-maturity, live as a whole being, whose inimitable strength rests in precisely the faculty to turn to the world not in a one-sided way through thinking only, but fully, with all the powers of feeling and willing intact.

Let us emphasize that we are not suggesting obstructing the development of the intellectual faculties. On the contrary, the intellectual faculties will receive a solid foundation when powerfully and securely embedded in a soul-life that is as rich and differentiated as possible. A young human being can only unfold the full spectrum of his faculties if all his faculties are developed. Only then will he be able bring these faculties to their highest manifestation and realization in his life.

## Individual and Community in the Artistic Process: In the Faculty

Educating the whole person through art should not be construed to mean that the first grade curriculum is exclusively artistic subjects. Subjects like arithmetic, foreign languages and grammar all have their place here, and they are taught in a way that affects the human being in its entirety. In other words, the artistic presentation of each subject is highly challenging and requires the teachers themselves to become learners and researchers, who pursue this path continuously. Routine would be the end of the art of teaching and educating.

If the individual teacher would have to undergo this continuous process of working on herself and self-transformation all alone and unaided, she would soon feel burdened. She receives support in the cooperation of her colleagues, who understand themselves to be on the same path of learning and researching. Mutual class visits have a refreshing effect and provide the teacher with reflections and new impulses for working.

Well-structured child studies can be particularly instructive and fruitful when all involved teachers share their unprejudiced observations about a child and earnestly strive to find ways to suitably support the child, if necessary, in cooperation with the school physician and school counselor. A specific institution in the Waldorf school is the weekly pedagogical faculty meeting, which is conducted in addition to the periodic class conferences. In these meetings those involved in the pedagogic work of the school try to expand their own pedagogic, psychological and methodic-didactic faculties. This sharing is the basis of the collegial work common at a Waldorf school. The quality of these meetings largely determines the pedagogical quality of the school. This is also true for Waldorf kindergartens.

## Individual and Community in the Artistic Process:
## In the Classroom

The mutual benefits of the individuals and the community working together are not only of value to the teachers, but also yield important tools for participation in artistically-taught classes. As the classroom teachers in the first six to eight grades generally teach most of the classes themselves, they can create a balanced rhythm between the individual student and the class as a whole. They can achieve this, on the one hand, through community-building arts such as singing, instrumental music, and choir recitals. Simultaneously the fine arts such as drawing, painting, sculpting work, and so forth, are given equal weight, depending on the developmental level of the class, supporting and increasing individual learning capacity at the same time as the social processes in the class community.

This breathing rhythm can also be realized through the medium of speech. Those less gifted are supported naturally by the more talented students when the entire class works together by speaking a poem in unison. Everyone notices his or her own efforts flowing into the whole and creating a shared achievement—all are happy in how they experience improvement day-to-day. But from time to time the individual child should step out from the community, for example by retelling a story or reciting a poem from memory, which the class teacher had written on his or her last report card as a companion thought for the school year. The class listens with interest to the saying the teacher has specially chosen or written for this child, and she respectfully accompanies the individual effort of the child, knowing how hard it is to recite something when standing in front of the class.

## Practical Instruction

Practical classes in a variety of subjects weave through all twelve grades, addressing the whole person in head, heart and hand. That includes needlework in the lower grades, working in the school garden or on a farm in the vicinity, as well as coming to know many traditional crafts such as masonry, blacksmithing, carpentry, shoemaking, and so forth. Increasingly, in our technically-oriented society, children lack the opportunity of balanced development, and such activities become more and more important—not because they satisfy a nostalgic need, but because they provide the children with lasting experiences of coherence. Such practical activities are an excellent means for empowering the children with courage to say yes to life. As the children come to experience basic work processes directly in a number of basic professions, not just reading about them or seeing them in a film, and as they perform this work themselves (as far as that is possible in showcase activities) the work world begins to appear to them as a cosmos of interwoven, mutually supportive processes. They can follow, for example, the path of the grain from the farmer's field to the baked bread on the breakfast table and can experience how each process builds on the previous one, how each profession needs the others—from sowing to harvesting, threshing and milling to baking.

This does not involve only the mind. As the children participate actively in each profession, they learn that a craft is an art that needs to be learned laboriously. They admire the expertise of the master, whose every grip "fits" the task and whose every work process is thought through so that useful things can be created. They do not have to hear that the world is formed by the abilities of man—they learn it "hands-on." Working in the garden or on a farm also allows them to experience a relationship with animals and plants, which a city child nowadays hardly ever gets to know. Yet such exposure is fundamental for a responsible relationship with nature and the environment; these experiences will accompany the person throughout his or her whole life.

Specifically organized class endeavors like the ones described above can give the young person a much more profound sense of belonging in this world, a feeling of trust and meaning, and the courage to make his own life decisions—much more so than words or pictures could ever do. These experiences nurture resilience, that invincible inner power that allows adults to take on and even master the crises in their lives.

**Fostering Movement**

In this time of cars and armchair media, the task of ensuring a post-maturation phase for the motor and sensory faculties falls more and more to education in the lower grades; a frighteningly high percentage of school

starters show insufficient or one-sided development. Many children no longer are able to stand on one leg, walk backwards or catch a ball. They can no longer develop even basic age-specific abilities like the kinesthetic, equilibrium and movement senses, let alone full mastery of their movement organism. Physicians and school admission officials can attest to that situation, bearing witness to a radical change in the conditions for healthy development. How are these children supposed to feel at home in the world if they cannot even truly inhabit their own bodies?

Modern brain research shows—last, not least—that the complete formation of the sensori-motor faculties is very important not only for the overall development of the child, but specifically for learning cultural skills such as reading, writing and arithmetic and for all cognitive processes. Since the plasticity of the brain has been shown to last a lifetime, much can be done in the school years to make up for what was missed earlier. Starting class with a practical exercise, engaging the whole class in rhythmical activities like stomping, jumping, running or clapping, can accomplish such compensation, in order to then strengthen the awareness and skill of coordinating hands and feet through appropriate exercises. Physical education classes, as well as activities like chopping wood, digging, baking, and so forth, offer rich opportunities for improving gross and subtle motor faculties.

Further opportunities can open up when a class works up a circus performance with balancing, acrobatic and artistic acts of all kinds. Children are easily motivated to continuously explore the limits of their abilities and expanding these limits through daily exercise. Cross-grade activities can emerge and grow easily into an all-school event, which can have an eminently pedagogical effect on many levels.

The subject of eurythmy is of particular importance in Waldorf schools for all grades. Eurythmy was created by Rudolf Steiner as a new discipline of movement, geared not towards the expression of one's own inner feelings but towards the congruent translation of language and music into corresponding gestures and movement sequences. At first, eurythmy was conceptualized as an on-stage performing art, making speech and music visible through the medium of the moving body, so-to-say time-elastic in space, with the audience experiencing the synergy [synaesthetics] of sound and movement, Melos and color moods, musical structure and movement choreography as a holistic work of art. But Steiner introduced eurythmy also as a core pedagogical curriculum subject because eurythmy requires that the powers of physical movement are harmoniously aligned with the powers of feeling and thinking, which alignment has positive formative effects on the whole person in body, soul and spirit.

Here more than in any other movement discipline, we can foster an integration of body and soul with the powers of the "I," altruistically and in

full service to speech and music emanating from fellow human beings. The challenges posed in eurythmy classes change and grow in correspondence to the respective developmental level of the children (Richter 2003).

## Individual Development and Developmental Divergences

As a College of Teachers works on ever more profoundly understanding the processes of human development, it becomes necessary to examine the efficacy of each subject and each teaching method in regard to supporting the respective developmental level of each class. What counts here is not the transmission of academic material, but whether or not the children's faculties are invigorated by a certain subject at a certain time through a certain methodology. In Waldorf pedagogy the age-appropriate way of teaching is so important that all children of one grade remain in the class—without being asked to repeat the class—until they reach the high school grades (with rare exceptions).

At the same time the teachers must recognize the special and unique development of each child. No two children develop exactly alike; the individuality always sets impulses that modify the general laws of development. Currently the range of developmental levels and processes seems to be growing even wider, which can lead to very divergent degrees of maturity in motor, intellectual, soul, and social faculties within one grade level. In addition, the tendency to dissociate is increasing, with most often the intellectual powers being ahead of soul and social faculties that are in need of catching up.

Therefore the development of each single child must be closely observed and individually supported as much as possible. Waldorf schools generally have a classroom teacher who, aided by the subject teachers, accompanies the children through many school years; he observes and supports them. This practice has over the years proven to be a very useful way for meeting that necessity.

On the other hand, certain changes in the way we teach are necessary due to the increase in developmental divergences and dissociations which present new challenges. Overall, there will have to be a much stronger emphasis on schooling sensory perception and fine-motor skills. An even stronger focus is required for language skills, which has already become a fundamental task for preschools and child care centers. But an increased effort must be made to continue to foster these skills far into the first years of school.

We also need to re-think the teaching environment for the first two or three grades. Classrooms have to be furnished ever more flexibly so that we can conduct the urgently needed remedial exercises in our daily practice. That is why more and more Waldorf schools are adopting the practice of only minimally furnishing the first grade classrooms, so that the children can readily engage in play or movement activities. Some schools even move certain parts of the class instruction to the outdoors in general.

The school yard has become more important; schools equip them with installations allowing free play and highly diverse elemental experiences that are otherwise hard to find for city children nowadays: climbing rocks and trees, balancing bars, sensory awareness paths, play houses, water ponds, craft workshops, stables for animal care, and so forth.

The opportunities for children to engage in free play should altogether be expanded, not only through suitable playgrounds and equipment for the break times, but also by working play sequences into the class itself, because here an essential part of remedial maturation can happen without stress. Supported by the adults, children can naturally explore and practice many different skills in their play activities: roles, boundaries and rules, problem solving, conflict resolution, respectful treatment of classmates.

The way we structure the schedule of a school day is also important. Pilot studies have shown that it is beneficial to abandon the rigid structure of forty-five-minute subject classes and to give the teachers the freedom to extend the individual phases of instruction or to shorten them as needed, until far into the morning and without depending on a break bell. That makes it easier for them to support individual children, brings more calm and breath to the class work, and allows the children to learn without stress.

**Fostering Rhythm throughout the School Year**

The conscious observance of daily, weekly, and yearly rhythms, of festivals and celebrations, is another important tool for harmonizing divergent developmental tendencies. Communal customs are seeded here, with stabilizing, harmonizing effects for the entire organization of body and soul, and these observances nurture the well being of the school and students alike. Rhythmic repetition (not to be confused with mechanical beat) is more important than ever in our hectic, jagged times, so that its health-engendering effects and developmental support are experienced by the children. That is already true for the time in kindergarten, but this educational approach proves beneficial also in grade school.

Waldorf education gives special consideration to the rhythm of night and day in the way it presents the subject material of a class in an open-ended way. The material covered in a day is not "finished"—the teacher refrains from offering a conclusion or final definition. Instead, the subject matter remains as concrete and colorful as possible in the outer and inner views of the students;

this openness is taken into the night. When the class resumes the next morning, memories of yesterday's experiences emerge, in distinctly transformed or condensed forms. One could say the soul has "digested" the subject material so that the feeling and willing parts of the person could integrate it. Now the students' questions have a very different level of depth and maturity than they could have reached on the previous day.

Modern research shows that learning continues into the night, yes, that the crucial deepening of information and experience that were taken in during the day are absorbed actually only at night, giving the night with its non-conscious nature an equally important role in the learning process as the day with its conscious awareness (Leber 1996). This also scientifically validates the Waldorf education principle of teaching a number of subjects in main lesson blocks. Block-teaching means that a general subject such as arithmetic or animal biology is presented as a focus of the morning lesson time for three to five weeks, taught each day for about ninety minutes, and then is not taught at all for a period of time. The fertile phase of "forgetting," which we see in the rhythm of day and night, also works over longer time frames.

Paying attention to such rhythms in conjunction with choosing age- and development-specific subject material fosters the common development of an age-homogeneous class community, without curbing the development of the individual child.

**The Nine-Year-Old**

A far-reaching change in the development of the young child occurs after the nine-year birthday, as sweeping as the transition from the kindergarten child to the school child. It is not marked by as dramatic symptoms as we will observe later with the start of puberty, and therefore it can easily be underestimated. But it is a preparatory stage to puberty and plunges the child into a crisis during which he needs much understanding and sensitive guidance from parents and teachers.

## Summary

An education oriented towards engendering health and sustainability, as sketched out in the previous sections, aims at ensuring that the adolescent develops and retains the ability of associating as a whole human being with events and challenges of his time, even after childhood, so that he can be sustained, even empowered, by the healthy accord of his somatic, emotional and cognitive abilities to act as an individual and to bring new impulses into the world.

The foundation for such a development must be laid already in childhood. The formative educational process does not start in school but already in the very first years of life. Education [the German word *Bildung* means education in the sense of "formative process" on both the mental and physical levels—trans.] has to be understood holistically and accomplished as a continuing process, whether at home, in kindergarten or in school, and the healthy development of the child is the focus.

However much the individual development may vary from child to child, their unfolding follows a fundamental law, which must be given particular consideration by educators and teacher in order to succeed in helping to form the whole person: the step-by-step metamorphosis of the formative powers, which at first act on the physical organization of the child and later transform into the formative powers for soul and mental/spiritual development. For example, in order to grasp the world, the physical ability to grasp must first be developed. The formative design of the physical organization, including in particular motor and sensori-motor faculties, creates the foundation for a healthy, sustainable unfolding of soul and mind activities.

The child must be given sufficient time to go through this process. If we try to advance intellectual activities prematurely, and thus engage the powers that are actually still needed for the formation of the physical organization, a weakening of the child's constitution and ability to achieve can ensue which may not become apparent until years later, depending on circumstances.

Waldorf pedagogy strives to foster health through education. Education as described here orients itself uncompromisingly toward the necessities for the child's development. Therefore it provides more than an acquisition of knowledge and skills. This education creates the basis for health for the individual's entire life span. In accordance with wellness research, health is understood as not just the absence of illness but the presence of an unfolding creative potential in body, soul and mind. Such development allows the human being to creatively shape his own fate and to grow ever more into becoming who he is: an individual with an unmistakable, unique signature mark. Such an individual will take initiative and play an active part in meeting the challenges of our world and will help shape the impulses of our future.

PART 2

GUIDELINES FOR THE EDUCATION OF THE CHILD FROM 3–9
AN OUTLINE OF A COMPREHENSIVE EDUCATIONAL APPROACH

# Foreword from the Original Edition

Early childhood has moved steadily into the focus of public interest. It is now recognized that the course of tomorrow's society is not set just during the school years, but already much earlier, in kindergarten and even before that during the very first years of life, when the child goes through experiences which can be pivotal for his entire life. "Education begins at birth." These words were coined by pedagogic researcher Gerd Schäfer, and consistent with their meaning, various political agencies have assigned high priority to public professional daycare institutions. The educational mandate of kindergarten has been fully acknowledged as being of prime importance, following just behind that for school education. New pathways for the transition from kindergarten to elementary school have been explored, and individual support for each child has become an imperative in the politics of education.

Meanwhile all States of the German Federal Republic have drawn up educational guidelines and orientation plans for kindergarten education, which are being tested in numerous facilities. Waldorf educators also feel committed to the essential goals laid down in these plans, yet intend to continue to realize these goals by different means.

In this time of restructuring and remodeling early childhood education, the International Association of Waldorf Kindergartens and the Association of Free Waldorf Schools in Germany deemed it necessary to take a stand and clarify the concepts and procedures of Waldorf education. This task was accomplished last year with the publication of the booklet *Guidelines of Waldorf Pedagogy for Children between Ages Three and Nine*, which outlines a salutogenic (health-engendering) education during kindergarten and the subsequent early school years, defining it as a process of continuous transformation which leads to lasting health and achievement only if the child is allowed enough time for going through the necessary developmental processes. This booklet received a positive response beyond the national scope, and translations into several European languages are currently in preparation.

In the following pages we present as a second step the systematic description of the educational goals, sectors *(areas)*, requirements and practices of Waldorf education for children ages three to nine. The teacher colleges of the German Waldorf kindergartens and Waldorf schools are in alignment with the contents of this paper. It is designed to determine the equivalence of the Waldorf-specific pedagogical concepts with the objectives of the public education and orientation plans issued by state agencies. We hope it will thus contribute to an equitable recognition of Waldorf education within the pluralistic German educational system.

We most cordially thank the team of authors and all our colleagues for their work reviewing this text and giving many valuable suggestions. We also want to thank all attentive editors, especially Wolfram Knabe, for their thorough proofreading of the manuscript.

We do hope that this second section will help to render the essential foundations and concerns of Waldorf pedagogy transparent and understandable, and that it will help in dealing with the public as well as government agencies and departments. Waldorf pedagogy's overarching concern is a comprehensive educational process for the young human being, stretching from birth to emancipation, from birth to age eighteen. Early childhood and the kindergarten and grade school years are viewed as stages within this continuous educational process. A next and third part of the "Guidelines" is planned which will address the years from birth to age three.

On behalf of the International Association of Waldorf Kindergartens and the Association of Free Waldorf Schools in Germany, we express our gratitude.

– Regina Hoeck and
Sylvia Bardt

# Goals of Education

**Respecting the Child's Individuality**

Waldorf education sees a unique, inviolable individuality in every child, regardless of his social, ethnic or religious background. This individuality existed before conception and birth and, from its past, brings a personal destiny with it into this present earthly existence, together with undisclosed talents that are not yet conscious to the child himself and which only gradually emerge later in life.

**Accompanying the Child into Freedom and Response-ability**

Education and training are meant to support the young person on his path towards self-discovery, so that he can find and unfold his latent inner abilities and intentions. The degree to which a person is successful in living and acting in harmony with his or her own goals, to that degree he or she is also free. That enables him to take on responsibilities of his own—not only for his own development but also for that of others, for the earth as a living organism and for the cultural and economic future of mankind. Education and training should support this path toward individual freedom and responsibility.

**Developing Social Competence**

Waldorf education aims to provide children and young adults with the capabilities necessary for fruitful activity within the social community. These competencies include respect for others, empathy, democratic awareness, moral discernment, joyous initiative and the willingness to take on responsibility and duty. In looking at the multicultural development of societies in our time, Waldorf education recognizes the important task of encouraging a non-judgmental interest in others of different cultural backgrounds so that openness and mutual understanding can occur. Children of both genders, coming from very different origins and with widely divergent talents, can live and learn in a climate of mutual respect and appreciation. This is true as well for children with special challenges, chronic illnesses and disabilities. In kindergarten the entire group benefits from educating such children together with all others; the integration of these children can also be a rewarding objective in school. In either case, the size of the group or class deserves attention; the development of positive social processes may be impeded and the success of the pedagogical efforts may be jeopardized if the class is not a manageable size.

## Engendering All-Round Good Health

A paramount objective of Waldorf education is to nurture and secure a stable basis for health, meaning not only the cultivation of physical foundations (for example, through healthy nutrition and sufficient exercise), but also the comprehensive harmony of the individual's organization in soul and spirit.

Engendering health, in the sense of salutogenesis, is considered to be an eminent pedagogical task, because the development of the child's good health is dependent in large measure upon factors for which adults are responsible. This includes the material and spiritual environments as much as the social behavior of teachers, their teaching methods, the learning atmosphere created through them, and much more. But health is also fostered within the context of a medical and therapeutic approach, as the Waldorf school concept from its beginnings incorporated therapists and school physicians as part of the college of teachers and who perform their work in closest contact with the teaching faculty and the parents. Especially medically prescribed therapeutic eurythmy has a firm place in many schools as do other therapies, such as therapeutic painting, modeling with clay, and music or speech therapy.

## Allowing Time for Lasting Development

In kindergarten and the grades, the foundation is laid for health or illness, for strength or weakness of achievement in later years, which places all pedagogical activity in a position of direct responsibility for the development of a person throughout his entire life. Therefore Waldorf education strives to allow the full and gradual maturation of all physical, intellectual and social powers and faculties of the young person. This provides the foundation for a lifelong ability to learn and achieve. The emphasis here is on a lasting, sustained development, not on speed. Each child must be given the time he needs for his own individual development.

## Holistic Education and Individual Support

In order to be certain that the growing child can unfold his or her individual impulses and abilities as freely as possible in later life, Waldorf education avoids every premature specialization and, with a broad-based and holistic approach, gives every child the possibility to develop according to his or her individual talents and predispositions. Teachers are supported in their efforts by physicians and therapists and strive for a close working relationship with parents and guardians. Many Waldorf institutions offer special support for children with learning difficulties or disabilities, even at times to special needs classes of their own.

## Overview of the Educational Process from Birth to Eighteen Years

Waldorf education recognizes the importance of understanding education and training as a process which begins already at birth and continues until maturity is reached at the age of eighteen. Therefore it strives to strengthen the cooperation between kindergarten and school and to realize a holistic educational process from birth to eighteen years, even down into the organizational structures. The text here at hand outlines a segment of that process by focusing on the life phase from three to nine years of age.

# Goals for Early Childhood Education

**Educational Mandate Particular to the Kindergarten**

Based on an understanding of developmental physiology and psychology, Waldorf education sees the task of early childhood and kindergarten education as being very different from the goals and tasks of the following  time of elementary school education. Reflective and intellectual capabilities are not at the forefront, but rather the main emphasis is on immersion in manifold, differentiated activities and concrete sensory experiences through which the child can expand and deepen his world of experience and perception through immediate, active participation; any challenges to faculties of intellect and mental reflection take a secondary role at this stage.

In this connection free play is of great importance. Imitation is fundamental to learning during this preschool and kindergarten age. For this reason the child's capacity for imitation is consciously stimulated and fostered through the activities of the adults and their behavior, because imitation is foundational at this age.

**The Particular Goals and Approach for Kindergarten and Preschool Education**

The child carries within himself a fountainhead of inexhaustible activity. He is a being who develops and forms from his own impulses. The child himself has a need to develop his sensory and motor abilities step-by-step so that he can move within the world and explore it—and he pursues this need with greatest intensity. In a manner of speaking, the child works himself into the world and thus develops his faculties.

However, since today's world no longer offers a child the appropriate quantity and quality of stimuli and opportunities for judgment that he needs to have presented in order for development to occur, an educational living environment for the child takes on increasing importance and significance. Parents and daycare centers (and later, the elementary schools) have the task of creating the outer and inner conditions that allow the child, from birth, to develop according to his individual possibilities and capabilities.

**Positive Learning Atmosphere and Reliable Relationships**

The loving attention of the adults, together with their willingness to build trusting and dependable relationships with the young being, are primary requirements for the child to thrive in body, soul and spirit. A positive emotional environment forms the critical matrix for healthy development, eagerness to learn, and interest in the world; consequently providing this environment is among the main creative tasks for all those who take part in the educational process.

**Adults as Role Models for the Children**

Regardless of his own faculty for autonomous development, the young child needs role models in all areas for imitation and orientation. The inner attitude and outer behavior of grownups form the first and most elementary learning environment whose imprint is left on the child's later biography. Parents and educators can fulfill this task of being role models through self-development and conscious reflection on their actions.

**A Foundation for the Authenticity of Personality**

If these basic conditions are met, the young human being can develop the instruments of his faculties in body, soul and spirit in ever more differentiated ways so that they become available to

him for realizing his intrinsic life goals. The striving of the individuality to live in harmony with himself and his own goals is a sensitive process that is susceptible to disturbance and disruption. It requires effort during one's entire life and may not always be successful. A goal of Waldorf education is to convey to the developing young human being the ability to meet the challenges of this process and to master them in such a way that the overall organization of body-soul-spirit can be rebalanced again and again; this enables him to develop creativity, the ability to handle stress, the courage for life, and a strong will for activity. Authenticity of the personality is the prerequisite for assuming true responsibility in selfless attention to the needs of other people, nature and the world.

**Engendering Coherence and Resilience**

Waldorf education is in alignment with the findings of salutogenesis research, which have determined that the foundation for human health is found primarily not in the biological realm, but in the person's faculties of soul and spirit necessary for meeting life's challenges. Coherence (the soul-connection with the world) is one of the most important of these faculties, as is resilience (the power to accept and master obstacles). These aspects are not hereditary gifts, but rather abilities for which education first creates a disposition and later in life the adult person can further develop through self-education.

## Good Health through Education

Didactically and methodologically, Waldorf education is designed to foster health. Health is understood not as simply an absence of illness, but rather as the presence of a creative potential for full development of the faculties of body, soul and spirit, which allows the human being to creatively and actively meet one's own destiny and consequently realize ever more one's own self as an individual with a unique, distinctive signature (mark) in the world. A healthy support for individual faculties also comprises the principle of refraining from setting a rigid learning pace from the outside; rather one must adapt the pace of the learning steps to the individual capacities of the child and his respective developmental age.

## A Foundation for Lifelong Learning and Achievement

In order to assure a healthy foundation for lifelong learning and achievement, Waldorf education places great importance on starting formal (in-school) learning only when the child can rely on a sufficiently developed physical organization, which can serve him as a dependable, resilient, strong

instrument. The forces active in building the organs and giving form to the physical organization (body) in the infant and toddler become available, though in a changed form, after about age seven as the forces of thinking and memory, used by the child now to form concepts and inner representations (images). Any premature employment of these powers for intellectual purposes detracts from the formation of the physical organization and can cause a long-lasting weakening of the bodily constitution.

## Allowing the Time for Maturation

School physicians and admissions counselors, as well as kindergarten teachers and childcare workers, are reporting more and more often dissociations in school readiness of today's children. Many children appear intellectually  ready for school, but physiologically, psychologically, and socially they are not. Waldorf education strives to provide, in kindergarten as well as in elementary school, the time and the means for these children to catch up on the maturing of abilities that have been hindered in their development. This applies also to deficits in speech development which we observe in more and more children.

## Developmental Metamorphosis and Age-Appropriate Learning

Waldorf education does not consider child development as a linear process, which would justify a training of skills for adult life as early as  possible. Rather, child development is seen as the consequence of independent phases, which figure as steps in a process of transformation (metamorphosis) and each requiring particular attention. This necessitates completely different conditions for the preschool and kindergarten ages than for the elementary school ages. Physical experience is the primary need of young children; the school child has needs of emotional and increasing mental interaction with the world. Implicit learning dominates the first phase, and the second phase is dominated by explicit learning. Waldorf education tries to incorporate all of these anthropological laws of development into the creation of the children's learning environment down to the smallest detail. The manner in which the adult addresses the child, too, should be distinctly different in these two phases.

**From Hand-Learning to Head-Learning**

Waldorf education is guided by the principle that the cognitive and intellectual abilities of the older school child are engendered by the earlier concrete activities of the young child, by acquiring coordination and through the active experiential participation in meaningful work- and life processes. First comes learning with the heart, hands, and feet; that is foremost during kindergarten and elementary school. Then comes learning with the head.

If the child is given ample opportunity, through direct bodily experience, to become familiar with the objects, processes, activities and facts of his life environment and to connect with them inwardly in the realm of feelings, then the child's experience of connectivity (coherence) is strengthened, and with it the basis for future joy of initiative, creative interaction with the world, zest for discovery, and capacity to learn. Therefore, it is the task of educators to form not only an inner sphere for development for the child, but also an outer sphere, so that the individuality, in a variety of ways and on all levels (physical, mental, and spiritual) is stimulated to activate his own powers.

**Relaying Ethical and Social Values through Active Role Models**

The pedagogical elements that provide a sense of experiential safety and inner stability include emotional attention from adults and also the relaying of ethical-moral qualities, the firm setting of boundaries and rules, adherence to good standards of behavior and conflict resolution strategies, as well as a natural relationship with one's own sexuality. In Waldorf education the preschool and kindergarten children are not taught through reflection and discussion, but by manifesting the desired qualities in adult role models so that they

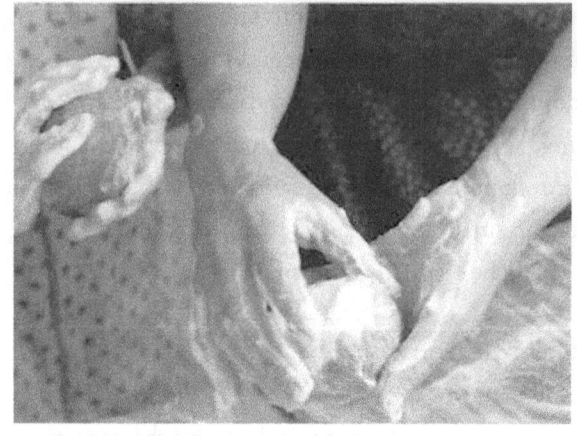are a living, natural reality which the child can take for granted and which he can then make his own through imitating them. The respect and appreciation, tolerance and sensitivity which an adult shows towards the child will have an immediate impact on the behavior of the child, and that behavior will become habit. In turn, the child expects rules to be obeyed and agreements kept. Through practical life experience, he learns what it means find his place within a community.

Waldorf education strives to strengthen the experience of social life through conscious cultivation of rituals, celebration of seasonal festivals, singing, making music, storytelling, and performing small theater plays. These practices also enrich and stimulate the experiential world of the child's soul. Concrete, pictorial presentations such as we find in fairy tales, legends, and small plays give the child an upwards glance into higher levels of human existence without verbal explanation, to the questions of where we come from, where we are going, and what is the purpose of life. These activities should always be brought in such ways as to consider what children from other cultures and religions bring with them and to learn about the traditions and religions through direct human encounter. Waldorf education is far removed from ideological indoctrination.

# Continuation into Elementary School

## School Is a Challenge

Starting school is a big challenge for all children because they encounter completely different conditions than were present in kindergarten. Learning is no longer exclusively accomplished through play, imitation, and participation within a time frame and to the degree that is tailored to each individual child (implicit learning). Now lessons are organized within the framework of a learning community that has certain tasks, goals and expectations (explicit learning). School learning is result-oriented and bound by certain time restrictions. School learning is a process of training and practice that requires the will to patiently perform repetitions. Activities become the subject of conscious reflection, and accomplishments are measured according to specific standards.

A further challenge lies in the size of the learning group, or class, which is now significantly larger than previously experienced by the child (family, kindergarten, childcare group). Now there are completely new social processes to be mastered. The right balance between accommodation and empathy on one hand and determination and self-assertion on the other hand must be found. The way a child meets these new challenges depends in large part on the conceptual method of instruction in the school and its practical application in the classroom.

## Preconditions for Goal-oriented Learning

In Waldorf education a key gauge for school readiness is the complete freeing up and transformation of the physical formative powers into those faculties that form the imagination and that allow for a conscious use of learning and memory capacities.  The forces of growth that the young child needs in the first phase of development for structuring the physical organization, after the partial completion of this organ-building activity, become available to the child to be used in a healthy way as forces of thinking, imagination, and memory. They are transformed into *consciously* available thinking and learning forces. Using these forces prematurely for intellectual pursuits prevents the maturation of the foundation of the physical organization.

The most noticeable sign of the end of this first phase of organ-building activity is the change of teeth (when the baby teeth are replaced by the permanent teeth). During this time, the young child's body, with its soft and chubby forms, changes into a more elongated, slender body build. The activity of the limbs becomes more coordinated, and often a child will display a preference for right- or left-handedness. Eye-hand coordination is developed to a stage ready for drawing, writing, reading, and so forth.

In a normal course of development, the sense of balance and movement should now be so far consolidated that a wide spectrum of purposeful movement sequences is possible (which previously were not reliably available), for example, jumping rope or walking backwards while keeping one's balance, actions that require new abilities in spatial orientation. Another aspect is the increasing ability to touch objects "blind" and be able to categorize them as things with which one is already familiar. If these faculties have reached maturity, they become the foundation for purposeful learning, reality-oriented thinking, the ability to recollect and memorize, and, last but not least, the kind of attention required in school.

If these faculties have not formed sufficiently, the result can be partial learning disabilities such as motor restlessness, lack of coordination, dissociation of movement sequences, and so on. That is why Waldorf education allows time in the elementary school for the formation, maturation (and sometimes retroactive maturation), and consolidation of physical competence, even though it is done in a totally different way than in kindergarten. At the root of this approach is the understanding that truly independent, self-initiated cognitive learning steps are based on experiences in physical and soul movement; otherwise these learning steps are just happening on a mechanical and outer level. Almost every learning process is based on this method: simple, *gripping* motions lead to more subtle, differentiated fine-motor *grasping* motions which lead to, finally, a comprehensive faculty of cognitive grasping or *understanding* on an inner level.

## Creating a Positive Atmosphere for Learning

What was said above, about the positive learning atmosphere for kindergarten-age children, applies equally for the school age levels: loving devotion from adults encourages and empowers the child so he can take the steps necessary to learn with joy and energy. Already through its organizational structure, Waldorf education facilitates reliable, stable bonds between child and teacher. Each class of children is led by a teacher who instructs daily and accompanies the children not only during the first years of school, but generally for six to eight years.

In the morning the teacher greets every single child, checking in with each of them personally through eye contact and handshake, and taking their

condition into account during the course of the day. During the first two years, the class teacher is also present during special subjects instruction and, as often as possible, he closes the school day with a shared time of review and concluding resonance. In these times of open and often changing family structures, the experiences of dependability and soul warmth in school are extremely valuable to the child. Along with educational support for physical skills, these add to the basic foundation for health and achievement.

## Preserving the Natural Joy of Life

Through its teaching methods, Waldorf education strives to foster and strengthen the natural joy of learning, with which the child enters school, in such a way that the child himself will preserve his will to learn even through occasional failure or setback. The child's experiences during the first school year are decisive: tendencies become apparent. Will the child experience learning as something oppressive that is forced upon him from the outside, or will the child continue with joy and willingness to learn, interested in and open to the world, forming the basis for lifelong learning?

In order bring about the latter, learning needs to take place in a warm, positive atmosphere that speaks strongly to the feeling nature of the child. Feeling qualities build bridges to the will forces. If a child enters into an instructional environment in such a way that he or she can turn to a subject with dedication and active interest, then the chances are good that the child's will forces can be engaged. Active, emotional experience is what makes it possible for a child  to connect with things as a whole person. Without this activation of the will, the interest will remain shallow and be short-lived.

## Developing and Strengthening Social Competency

Waldorf education in elementary school—in contrast to the kindergarten—attributes great value to an age-homogeneous community in which the child lives and learns throughout the grades. This is seen as a key factor, enabling the school to properly involve and support the children and adolescents according to their ages and respective developmental levels. The class community encompasses (because of the distribution of birthdays in any given year) not only younger and older children, but also children of widely divergent backgrounds and talents. The development of social competency is ensured by this approach as well as by the fact that there is no grading and no repetition of a class in Waldorf schools. From the beginning, the children learn that the issue is not success or failure, but how all persons can bring their special capabilities and qualities to the community as a whole. This understanding evokes in them a natural mutual respect, and everyone offers to help everyone else to the best of their abilities. Naturally, in the course of daily encounters, there are conflicts to be resolved, aggressions to be overcome, and the need to accept others with all of one's strengths and weaknesses.

Waldorf education tries to stimulate and foster direct awareness and true understanding of the other human being—not only through its social structure but also through its teaching methods. In particular, the field of artistic-musical instruction offers rich opportunities for practice. "Listening to each other" is a consistent topic throughout all the school years.

# Capacities Developed in Kindergarten

## 1. General Principles

Waldorf education strives to foster comprehensive development of capabilities for which the child is predisposed. This is accomplished through simultaneous perception and respect for the rights of personality of each child. It orients itself on physiological and psychological developmental factors that are present in each age group, modified by special, individual characteristics.

Learning in the kindergarten is implicit in nature. It comes about through full immersion in activities that come out of the immediate perception of the environment, without reflection. It is the nature of a young child to exhibit unreserved dedication to his sense impressions, and make an active connection to he world surrounding him. This means, however, that at this age all learning is a complex and holistic process which cannot be subdivided into different "subjects." While we will nevertheless refer in the following text to specific

educational areas, it must always be kept in mind that in real life these areas never occur just by themselves; they also cannot be fostered in isolation from each other, but the various areas of instruction overlap and intermingle in manifold ways. For example, in the activity of baking bread, aspects of health and nutrition play a role, but also motor skills are schooled through the activity of kneading the dough, mathematics is introduced through measuring the ingredients and the weight of the finished loaf of bread, and the ability to form thought images of a physical process, such as baking, is further developed. Add to that the planting, care, harvesting, threshing, and grinding of the grain, and the child experiences a sensory connection between his perceptions and his own activities. This provides the child with a sense of coherence.

This is particularly true in the area of ethical-religious education, which should be present in all activities and creative endeavors with the children. Here the focus is not on any particular content, but on whether the adult is able to authentically model a basic attitude of reverence and to be a living example of devotion and love as a life path. It is not abstract knowledge but

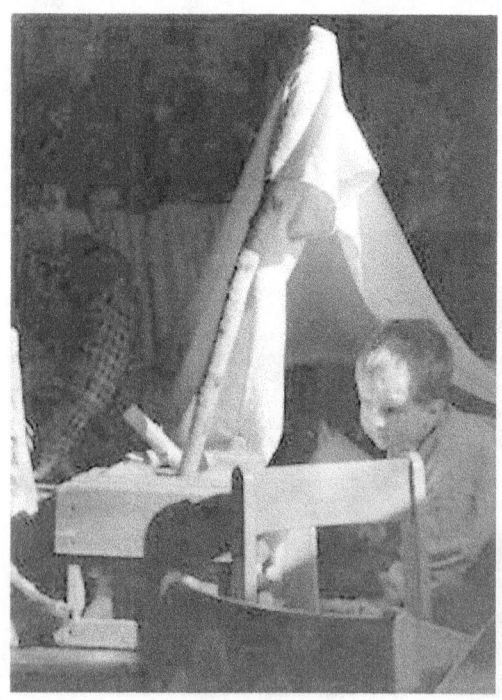

the true experience of such ethos and attitudes which exerts a deep moral influence on the young child. Waldorf education endeavors to provide the experiences of coherence and the development of resilience to the fullest extent of which the individual child is capable by allowing the children to immerse themselves in a wide variety of reality-filled activities that have a connection to daily life. Especially in our times, when children are afforded fewer and fewer opportunities for hands-on experiences, an approach like this is of great value.

Instead of introducing the world to the child through technical media, these immediate experiences stimulate and challenge the child's own joy of discovery and activity and strengthens his capacity for self-development. Waldorf education likewise finds it necessary to foster the faculties of thinking, reflection and intellectual discrimination to come in later years precisely through explicitly *not* challenging these faculties in the preschool and kindergarten levels. The realities surrounding the child and created by adults and the relationships in the child's environment are the means by which a child is self-taught. The child teaches himself, stimulated by the facts and conditions of his environment provided (created) by the adults.

Only after reaching a certain developmental stage towards the end of the first seven-year cycle do conscious reflection and thought activity take their due place in the learning process. The instruction is the same for boys and girls alike. Each child of his or her own accord gleans from the rich pedagogical options that which corresponds to his or her own leanings, while the educator supports this choice. The way Waldorf education deals with the child's sexuality and with questions of sexual education is the topic of a different publication (Maris/Zech, 2006, see bibliography).

## 2. Free Play as an Activity that Fosters Development

The play of the young child differs distinctly from that of the older child, and even more from that of the adult. We would fall prey to a deep misunderstanding if we regarded "play" as a form of "leisure activity." For young children, play is work, through which they make the world their own. For this reason, Waldorf education pays great attention to childhood play. There is no other activity that affords the child such an opportunity for self-education. All life skills can be thoroughly investigated and practiced—from varied motor and sensory skills up to all life competencies and social skills.

Free play is also a perfect basis for developing their own individuality. As the child lives earnestly in his play, so will he in later life be able to immerse himself into his work. The only difference between the child's play and the adult's work is that work integrates itself into the outer purposefulness of the world, but the play of the child arises from impulses that emerge from within and are free from purpose-orientation.

The kind of free play under consideration here remains uninfluenced by instructive or interruptive interventions of the adults. Also the toys and

play materials should predetermine the play activity as little as possible, so that the child can imbue the things of the world with meaning from within and can be fully immersed in the creative fantasy of the moment. He can practice being autonomous, sovereign and free, because he acts solely from inner motivation and determines for himself the values and rules of the play. The child has the opportunity to grasp what he experiences daily in his environment using his own will and to process these experiences creatively through imitative activity, thereby making these
experiences his own. Even traumatic experiences, hindrances, aggression and fear can be dissipated and transformed through play into positive faculties.

**Forms of Play**

The particular nature of free play changes with each age level, mirroring the developmental process of the child. In the first two years of life, the child discovers his own body through play. Children feel their hands and feet and test their motor skills. Eye-hand coordination and left-right coordination are constantly refined. As soon as the child can walk, he finds the greatest pleasure grasping all the things in his environment, touching and exploring them. He imitates the movements he has perceived by observing the gestures and activities of the adults working around him. His own joyful activity awakens in him a sense for the meaning of things and their interconnectedness. Any effort to teach the child the purpose of his activity would likely distance him from this connection, rather than further a close, spontaneous immersion, which is characteristic of the unconscious way of learning in the first years of life.

From ages two to four, when the child is able to move about more freely, there is a marked change in play behavior. With a seemingly unending treasury

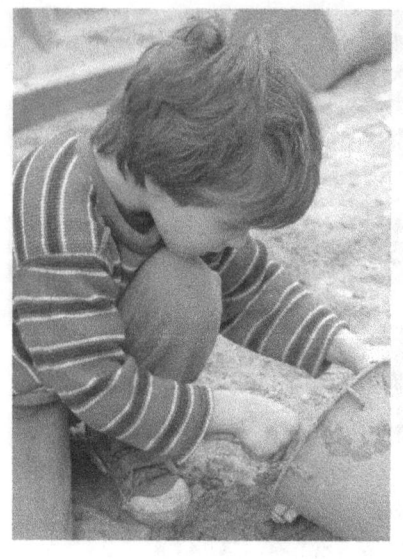

of ideas, the child will dispense with the predetermined purpose of an object and give it a surprising, new, and completely different one. For example, a spoon will suddenly be a telephone. A footstool becomes a motorcycle, a doll's bed, a train car, or a cooking stove.

But it is not only the way in which a child plays with the things that has changed. The play process itself takes on ever-new forms as the impressions from the child's surroundings begin to provide the motivation. Objects and events in his environment offer welcome opportunities to the child for using his powers of imagination. He wants to transform, supplement, create anew, and go beyond that which is given. His horizon expands continuously in this process, perceptions coalesce with feelings and thoughts, and a web of meaning begins to unfold. He begins to understand.

From ages five to six, there is another significant and noticeable change in play behavior. While before age five it was outer impressions and events that stimulated play, now, increasingly, the promptings are internal, from the pictures of the child's own imagination and memory. Now thought precedes will; the child first makes plans and then executes those plans. The play materials are the same, but now the child wants to make sure that his imagined world is completely like the real world. He will declare the things he is playing with to be "real." For example, a small broom may be stuck through the handle of a basket, wrapped around with string, and transformed into an outboard motor that "really works" when the broom turns (when the string is pulled).

At this age level play becomes more social and continuous. Entire action sequences are remembered, recalled and reenacted. The children assign themselves roles and adhere to rules that they have created. Such themes of play can go on over a period of days. Often the children already know what they are going to play before they arrive at kindergarten that day.

## Building Ethical and Moral Values through Free Play

Willing, feeling and imagination can develop in a healthy way and be deeply interconnected if the child is given sufficient time and space for moving through the play phases outlined above. The child learns not only to stay true to his own impulses emerging from within and to actively make them a reality; he also learns to feel what he wills and does and to understand ever more clearly the consequences of his actions. The first seeds of morality and prudence come to life engendered by the earnestness of free, creative play. Freedom together with personal responsibility, creative fantasy and an awareness of rules can grow from here, as do competence and consideration. The seeds for fundamental social and moral faculties are sown to unfold in later life.

## Play Facilitation through Adults

In order to stimulate such content-rich play, the child needs adequate time, a quiet, positive atmosphere, and play materials taken from nature, which do not define the play through any purposeful directive. Such play also needs an environment in which the adults engage in meaningful, practical tasks of life, so that the children can see and experience the meaning and process of these activities. This encourages imitation and awakens the urge to play, while scripted activities or learning programs just cut into the time for free play and hinder the unfolding of true individual, creative initiative.

# 3. Movement, Physical Development, and Health

## Pedagogical Aspects

Constantly in motion, active with the whole body and all the senses, the young child connects to his world. In no other phase of life do movement and sensory experience have such significance as in the first few years of life. Every activity—whether motoric or sensory in nature—works its way into the neurological structure of a growing child. Continuous movement strengthens the faculties for physical control and thus lays an important cornerstone for a positive body sense, healthy life processes and an expressive faculty of soul.

The experience of the world and self receives its foundation here and affects the entire course of life.

## The Motor and Physical Development of the Child

During the first and second years of life the child takes ownership of his body. He begins with eye coordination and control of head movements, then comes playing with the hands and later with the feet, then rolling, scooting, crawling, standing upright, and walking. Along with these intense, though unconscious, sensorimotor achievements of the child, we see a maturation of his sense-perception organs and structures of the nervous system, forming the basis for the abilities to speak and think. Up to the age of five, the child becomes more and more adept in balancing: he can climb stairs, walk for a considerable time, hop, jump, dress and undress. By employing increasingly conscious perception, the child purposefully exercises his motor faculties, clear down to the tips of his toes and fingers. For example, now the child commands enough dexterity to tie a bow or thread a needle. The arches of the feet, the curvature of the spine and the rounding of the ribcage are taking form, and rhythms of heartbeat and breathing stabilize.

In the sixth and seventh years of life, the child gains increasingly differentiated fine motor skills and coordination of his arms, hands, legs, and feet. The entire body becomes surer in movement and balance. The limbs become more elongated and change proportion in relation to the rest of the body. These phenomena are visible expressions of the ever-increasing maturation of the central nervous system and, along with it, of consciousness. Faculties of spirit and soul are growing. Observing the motor and physical development of the child can be helpful to educators so they can provide the appropriate stimuli for continued development or therapeutic help in cases of difficulty or delay. Furthermore, the observation and assessment of bodily maturation can be helpful in determining school readiness, since to the same degree that the body matures, the forces of soul and spirit are released to facilitate the transition from implicit to explicit learning.

This developmental process also finds expression in children's drawings. The themes depend upon the child's age, but the drawings are the same for children all over the world. When the drawings are created in an atmosphere of freedom, without direction, and truly out of the inner impulses of the child, they contain certain universal patterns which can help us assess the developmental level.

## Formation of Ethical and Moral Values through Movement

Only movement with meaning and purpose is of formative value for the development of the child. Pointless romps and frenzied activity have rather negative effects and are not suitable for structuring the brain. For this reason, it is of critical importance for the young child to perceive movement in adults that is internally driven and mentally enlivened so that when he imitates those kinds of movements, he can differentiate his own movement-organism and develop it into full functional capacity. Joy, strength, confidence, as well as competence to act, and tolerance for frustration grow within the child through these activities and allow the growing person to meet the world with a positive attitude and to work in the world in a meaningful way. At the same time, the child's moral sense is strengthened. The gestures and movements, facial expressions and body language of the adult are read by the child as unmistakable indicators of the attitudes which are at the core of the adult's behavior. However much the adult may try to conceal negative motives, the child can perceive in the actions any discrepancy between outer pretense and inner reality. The child's sense for honesty is active long before he will consciously ponder questions of morality.

## Adult Support for Motor Development

If the child is given enough space for movement and time for uninterrupted play, building and "working," then his motor development will proceed in a healthy way. A fundamental condition is that the child is allowed to go through each of the developmental steps and experiences at his own pace, in accordance with his individuality. The loving attention of adults strengthens the harmonious formation of the child's energy sources.

Repetitive rhythmic processes and meaningfully ordered activities are of further help. Regularity and repetition exert an organizing, structuring influence on the physical development of the child. For this reason, the Waldorf kindergarten places a high value on daily and weekly rhythms and on recurring activities: finger- and hand-games, circle games, rhymes and songs in which the children can participate or imitate later. In eurythmy the child moves according to the patterns set by verses, rhythms or melodies and joyfully integrates the gestures of the teacher; he thus trains his own skill while moving toward an inner-directed gesture of his own.

Other regular activities include watercolor painting, drawing with wax crayons, beeswax modeling, handwork, and helping with household tasks such as washing, baking, cutting fruit, and gardening. Indoor and outdoor play and outings to the forest, for example, in all weathers, provide a variety of routine opportunities for movement experiences and practice.

# 4. Speech Development

## Pedagogical Aspects

Language and speech mean more to the human being than just a means for communication. They are the most important basis for our social life; they give us the possibility to share with each other what moves us within. And even moreso, through language, the connectivity of meaning and purpose become apparent, the cosmos of thoughts receives structure. Questions emerge concerning the origin and destination of the human being, the "why" of things and processes, and these questions can only be asked and answered through the medium of speech.

The development in fine and gross motor skills, as described in the previous paragraphs, forms the physical foundation for the child's learning to speak. Just as the child could not learn to walk upright without seeing the model of walking adults, so he needs adults for learning to speak. Nonverbal communication makes up by far the largest aspect of speech, and the child depends not only on what he hears in tone, pitch and rhythm but also on

what he sees in the subtle aspects of gesture, facial expression and demeanor of those speaking. For this, children need adults who devote sufficient time and attention to them. Much research has proven that learning to speak happens only during live interaction, person to person; technical media cannot assume this task. The mutual listening and speaking process is the precondition for any development and fostering of speech.

**Phases of Speech Development**

When the infant first starts to interact with his world, he has already begun to acquire the elements of speech. Gesture, pitch of voice, the facial expressions of those human beings around him all give the infant opportunities to explore the meaning of the sounds and tones he perceives, long before he can actually produce these sounds himself.

Speaking is learned through a highly complex process of fine-motor and muscular control in which the regulation and rhythm of breathing play an important role, just as does the complicated synergy of larynx and speech musculature in the head, facial expression and body language. This process continues well into school age. The larger the vocabulary and the more precise the language usage, then the more deeply and richly can the child express his own thoughts and feelings

At the same time the mastering of speech lays the groundwork for freeing up the thinking faculty, which can then grow beyond the scope of language. It has been shown that from infancy children have an astounding ability to unconsciously perceive structural patterns and laws of the language in their environment and to anchor them in their brains. Acquiring the ability to form sentences of their own and to express increasingly complex content, they obviously "know" the rules of language without ever having learned them consciously. It is only later, when the child is in school, that the rules and patterns of language, its grammar and syntax are brought step by step into the light of consciousness, and especially in the context of learning foreign languages. Learning to write and read prepares the child for this highly abstract achievement in language development. Translating the life-resonant acoustic phenomenon of speech into graphic signs demands the conscious effort of the child, just as this is necessary for the reverse task of transforming the visual symbols into speech and meaning.

## Fostering Ethical and Moral Values through Language

Language not only offers the child the opportunity to express his own thoughts and feelings, but also in growing measure the child can begin to perceive the world, the thoughts and feelings of other people and unfamiliar cultures. He can enter these new horizons, build human relationships, and learn to understand others in their different, unique states of being.

Language forms a sense of morality and love of the truth in a child because he learns that every word has a certain meaning, a certain sense. The child instinctively expects a specific action or reaction to take place with certain word usage; words and deeds match. Our attitude (ethos) and truthfulness are extremely important when we speak with children. Children do not understand irony or sarcasm. This developing capacity of speech must mature for the child to be able to see through an intentional lapse between what is said and what is meant and understand it as a joke or witticism.

## Stimulation of Speech Development by the Adult

Rich verbal communication with the child naturally fosters his ability to learn to speak, especially when the adults clearly articulate their words and meanings. The congruency of their words with their body language and gestures is perceived and tested by children. This requires a high measure of self-discipline from adults. But patience in listening to the child is equally important and to let him finish talking so that he can gather thoughts calmly, formulate them into words and sentences, and express his thoughts and concerns without haste or pressure. One should exercise such attentive communication many times throughout the day—during greeting, play times and mealtimes. The child should be addressed so that vocabulary use and content are appropriate for his age, neither "over his head" nor in a childish way or in "baby talk."

Pictorial, imaginative language that draws on the child's own imagination is of great importance for the cultivation of language. There are many rhymes and poems, dances and circle games to be found in the Waldorf kindergarten and in eurythmy. Language, music and movement are harmoniously blended so that the whole human being is involved. Daily stories and fairy tales not only enrich the vocabulary and language skills of the children who listen, but at the same time they activate the imagination and creative powers. As in every learning process, it is important to tell and retell the same themes time and again, or demonstrate them in puppet play, so that the children can get fully involved with the content and the presentation. They take joy in recognizing what they have seen and heard before. With the security of association, they can take on more challenging language and imaginatively integrate what they have heard into their play activities.

# 5. Artistic Development through Rhythmic and Musical Education

## Pedagogical Aspects

Children are born artists. They joyfully engage in activities, employing their creative faculties and stand so-to-say in the midst of life through their active work. They enter into the essence of things unconsciously, while we adults are rather more onlookers, observers and critics, keeping our distance. Our causal-logical and scientific-conscious thinking forms a polarity to the creative energy of the child.

The art of education consists of leading young human beings into a conscious understanding of the world without losing their creative potential or individual formative powers. This needs time. All kinds of artistic activities are invaluable, as long as the adults are willing to learn to become artists themselves.

## Cultivation of Music and Rhythm

In today's daily family life, and also in school, there is less and less singing done with children. This intrinsic human activity needs to be especially attended to nowadays. Recent scientific findings show that singing is not only a matter pertaining to human sentiment; more importantly, it strengthens the child's health, deepens breathing, and supports the maturation of breathing and speaking organs.

In singing, as in all musical activities, rhythm is of particular importance. It has an ordering, stabilizing effect on the organization of the child's body, soul and spirit. At the same time, the child builds on his prenatal experiences, during which time he was constantly under the influence of his mother's heartbeat, breathing, gait and movements. The rhythms of speech are perceived already before birth, and newborns are familiar with them long before they can learn to speak. Rhythm connects speech, music and movement, and this threefold aspect should thread throughout childhood as one element of life.

The time in kindergarten offers a myriad of opportunities to implement this mandate daily, as the children sing songs, recite verses and imitate the adults' movements to illustrate the content. They make the effort, without having to be prompted, to improve the precision of their movements and gestures. For example, we practice big, stomping steps alternating with slight, tripping steps, or we gallop like little horses and then abruptly come to a halt when the verse or music ends. Without any direct verbal instruction, the children acquire complex sensorimotor skills which give them a deep sense of satisfaction and at the same time further their development.

**Formation of Ethical and Moral Values through Music**

Music leads to the harmony of the soul and to an even temper; it fosters cognitive development, joy of movement and vitality. It strengthens self-assurance in life and stabilizes the personality. Musical-rhythmic activity is an ideal path for stimulating the creative imagination of children and their powers of initiative. But music is not only a guide inwards to one's own self; it also leads us outwards into the world. By experiencing the quality of sounds, tones, melodies and rhythms, the child gains insight into the essence of things; he can touch the sphere of genuineness and truthfulness. Likewise social relationships are strengthened, because listening, becoming attuned to each other, and creating harmonious sounds are activities that give rise to an integrative group life, in which every participant makes an indispensable contribution through the power of his or her individuality. Scientific research has shown that making music together not only fosters musical ability but also increases social competency.

**Artistic Activities in Kindergarten**

Interconnected elements of speech, rhythm and music permeate daily life in the Waldorf kindergarten. The children sing songs, play simple instruments such as child's harp, xylophone, sounding bells; they speak verses and rhymes, adding finger- and hand-gesture games, and every day they hear stories or fairy tales, either read or told to them.

The eurythmy class, taught by a professional eurythmy teacher, forms a special highlight of the day or week. Eurythmy is a movement art form in which speech and movement are realized concurrently through gestures and movement sequences. The physical movement training here is inextricably linked with a training of inner soul movement and of the powers of sensitivity and emotion, along with an increase in spiritual presence, so that this art can have a forming effect on the whole person moreso than any other branch of the arts. Eurythmy is not yet as systematically practiced in kindergarten as later in school, but it relies entirely, simply and age-appropriately on imitation and action.

Circle time is another period of condensed artistic activity led daily by the class teacher. Songs and verses through the seasons are sung, played, and explored through various appropriate gestures. Hearing and seeing, feeling and imagining, moving and acting are all intertwined and fuse into one integral whole through the child's participation, which helps the child's constitution clear into his or her physical body. Speech, movement, and music are all present at the same time. The children practice social skills when they find their place in a formation, or do something in pairs or alone, or when they wait and watch. The age diversity of the group supports this holistic education. The older children act as models because they know the movements and songs from the previous year and can already perform even complicated sequences. That strengthens their self-confidence and gives the younger ones an incentive to imitate them. The play with dolls and hand puppets is also important. It provides an extraordinary stimulus for the child's powers of imagination and fosters aesthetic faculties as well as dexterity.

Concentration and purposeful activity are effortless corollaries of entering the experience of the process. Children react with the same intensity as they listen to fairy tales. The pictorial language evokes in them a colorful world of inner images which vividly melds with the powers of feeling, will and soul, and they absorb these tales like nourishment for the spirit. Listening to audio cassettes or disks cannot take the place of live singing and storytelling. Children need the connection and relationship with a real person in the same room with them in order to go from the example, or role model, to their own activity. It is not necessary that the adult possess great musical or rhetorical talent. What counts for the children is not an adult's ability but the effort that is made in singing or storytelling.

Modeling with beeswax is another artistic activity through which the children experience the formative power of their hands and the effects of warmth processes, pressure and counter-pressure. They experience corners and flat surfaces, various forms and how they transform in space. Painting with watercolors is a very joyful activity in kindergarten—in movement, transformation, bonding, and encountering and mixing of colors. At this age there are no specific themes given, so the children paint or draw with spontaneity. Any correction, judgment, or reflection can create distance that will obstruct the children's inner will to create and their imagination.

Children of kindergarten age are all about the activity, not the result. They live in the moment, in the immediate activity and in the fulfillment of the present.

# 6. Foundations of Mathematics and Science Education

## Pedagogical Aspects

Children are very interested in all phenomena in nature. Curious, inquisitive, exploring and testing, they approach the world—not with scientific and critical reflection but with spontaneous activity and sensory perception. What they experience enters their play. If we observe carefully, child's play is revealed to be excellent unconscious preparation for future education in mathematics and natural sciences, provided this play can proceed freely and without an adult agenda. When children handle natural materials they naturally build and construct, sort and order, compare and try. They unconsciously, but directly through their senses, experience mass, weight, quality, and quantity. They investigate the sensory world and learn how to interact with it. Long before they can calculate with numbers or the laws of physics, they are mastering, almost imperceptibly, the basic skills in mathematics and science, thereby laying the groundwork for their abilities in those fields of study. Everything that can later be known and understood with the mind is first experienced with the physical senses.

## Laying the Foundation

The young child lives always in the present moment, centered in his own experience. Only slowly does an awareness of "yesterday" and "tomorrow" unfold, based on the experience of "now" and "today," and giving rise to understanding life as extending into the past and the future, thus developing the faculty of conscious memory. A prerequisite for such development is that the child live in daily, weekly and yearly rhythms which the adults consciously structure to recur in similar patterns. The child experiences time and space by way of structure, regularity and quantity; he is not yet able to objectively experience and judge amounts and proportions. His consciousness slowly awakens to grasp the qualities of space and time, of quantity, number and geometric laws in correspondence to his physical development. That is why the healthy formation and maturation of the sensory organs and their functions,

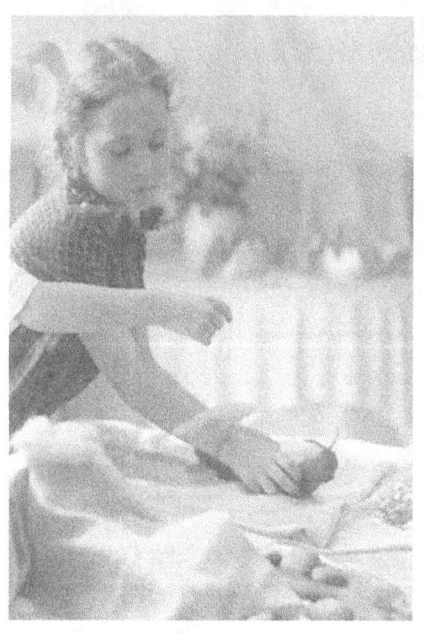 as well as the movement organism, are a top priority of preschool and kindergarten education, extending into the first few grades of elementary school.

Through their activities the children come to know the properties, qualities and patterns of their environment. For example, coming to stand upright and learning to walk are experiences of gravity and spatial dimensions. Later, similarly, the child bodily experiences momentum and buoyancy, gravity, centrifugal force, friction, and so forth, when he jumps rope, plays on the swings, merry-go-round, teeter-totter or slides. He can comprehend these principles and transpose them into his play, when, for example, he lets chestnuts roll down the slope of a wooden board or when he builds runways for marbles or bridges and towers. In this process he also explores the laws of leverage, stasis and balance.

During eurythmy and in circle time, the children unconsciously experience through their own movements the geometric concepts (and the actual forms) of the circle and the center, ovals, lines, and spirals as well as inside/outside, above/below, and right/left. Spatial imagination is trained in this process as well as a sense for proportions.

The connections and associations that the child experiences through play, through experiments with the play materials, and through the use of his entire body coalesce into a still-unconscious physical-kinesthetic intelligence. This builds the foundation for the exacting, mathematical and scientific thinking and understanding in later life. Around the time of the change of teeth the child has the capacity to deal rationally with the concepts of space and time. At that time the child can recognize and think about something as a physical law that had been experienced physically and tested in play during his first six years of life.

## Formation of Ethical and Moral Values

When children experience adults regarding the phenomena of nature in wonder, when they see how their teachers meet all that lives with respect, joy and reverence, a deep sense of responsibility takes root in them, a sense for morality. An inner certainty ripens that the forces and relationships governing nature also govern human thinking. The children experience the world as reliable and ordered by law, and thus they gain trust in their own existence  and a positive mental outlook towards their environment. They regard the world as a place where they feel at home. It is fundamentally important that children experience the world as a good and well-ordered place in their first few years of life because this will give them the basis and the strength they need to meet life's dangers and problems.

## The Daily Kindergarten Routine

The daily routine in kindergarten offers manifold opportunities for dealing with laws of mathematics and physics without bringing them into conscious awareness through reflection. The children deal with quantities and numbers, for example, when they set the table, cut an apple into segments, measure ingredients for baking, or count the number of muffins. Factual logic and systematic procedures are promoted purely through their everyday activities, for example, when they tidy up after free play, when they sort the materials they used and put them in their proper places. Besides creating order on the outside, this also creates internal order and promotes the capacity for overview, as well as independence.

In outside play, the children learn how different things feel when they touch sand, clay, water, wood, stone, and so forth. The qualities of hard/soft, rough/smooth, and warm/cold become immediate realities through hands-on experience. Children also observe how sand and clay are different when they mingle with water, or that leaves and wood swim while little stones sink to the bottom when thrown into water.

Working in the garden, walks and small excursions into the park or forest offer opportunities for coming to know plants, to track their growth, blossoming and wilting. The children can observe animals and rainbows and clouds; they become aware of the daily rhythm, the course of the sun, the changes in daylight, warm and cold weather through the seasons. Much is gained towards a development of an understanding in the natural sciences when the child of this age learns not through dry abstractions, but enters immediate, soul-satisfying experiences drawn from the inexhaustible treasury of the sensory world.

This level of activity preserves a sense of wonder and creative curiosity way into the school years, when the child will need to enter also into an intellectual understanding of things, and when that rational, thinking element meets the foundation of perception that was laid in kindergarten and now assures that the emerging human being can make a connection to the world not only through his head, but also with his whole being: head, heart, and hands.

# 7. Formation of Social Skills

## Pedagogical Aspects

There is one essential prerequisite to the formation of social competency. To develop empathy and understanding for others, the child must first be able to experience and express his own independent individuality; he must feel acknowledged and accepted by his fellow human beings. The degree to which the child experiences being safe and held securely in reliable human relationships is the degree to which he develops feelings of self-worth and independence. Only on this basis can he become free to not only look at himself but also turn to others with interest, respect and a willingness to help.

## Developmental Steps towards Social Competency

At first the infant knows only his own needs and expects complete attention. Nothing is better for him than being embedded as early as possible into an existing and very stable social situation. The toddler is still in great need of relationships; without a dependable attachment figure, he cannot thrive. The young child lives in the trust that others are there for him who unwaveringly care for him, who help him. Having this trust fulfilled is the prerequisite for the child's developing social competencies. Only in the course of time will the child become independent enough to experience himself as separate from his environment and to become aware of the needs of others.

On this path towards social competency, the child has already made the first steps when, coming from the small community of the family, he now enters into the larger, unfamiliar community of the kindergarten. In the mixed-age group, the child meets both younger and older children with whom he needs to come to terms. Manifold social experiences open up to the child here, especially for children without siblings. On the other hand care is taken that the child can experience safety and warmth in this new, larger community. The group structure remains the same over a long period of time, which allows the child the space and time to pass through his individual steps of development in a circle of trusted people and a familiar environment and to form stable relationships with other children and the teacher. A rhythm of activities through the week and the regular celebration of seasonal festivals give the child an overview of schedule and time. This all creates a sense of trust in the world and in people, thus forming the basis for a growing social competency.

The phase of development known as the "terrible twos" is the child's initial attempt to become independent of the persons he is attached to and whom he trusts. The child explores and tests his autonomy and becomes conscious of his own powers of will. At the same time, the child can learn in the protected space of the kindergarten, build relationships with a wider circle of people, and shape, enjoy and accept common life in a larger group of children. The child

learns to be considerate and to wait; he experiences how older children can help him. A mixed-age group proves to be a natural aid on the path towards social aptitude, especially during the last year before elementary school, when the "big ones" are familiar with the kindergarten routines, so they can be models for the younger ones. They are confident of their ability and knowledge, so they can naturally take on tasks and give guidance to the younger children. A sense of responsibility develops along with perseverance and an earnest attitude towards work in conjunction with self-assurance and strength. Thus the younger children are motivated to become just as capable later on. For the children in their last year of kindergarten there should be special tasks that afford them opportunities to take on responsibility, to prove their skills and perseverance, and to meet their desire to be of assistance to other human beings in a purposeful way. Special projects, field trips and challenging tasks are suitable for this purpose.

The progression from kindergartner to school child is characterized by a fundamental change in social relationships as well as in learning behavior. Explicit learning takes the place of implicit learning, and the child is now in a group of approximately the same age and level of development. Where before, routine and unconscious habits lent stability and boundaries to the child, now this function is imparted through rules and direction from a recognized and beloved authority figure. The child can now consciously acquire social skills through practice.

**Formation of Ethical and Moral Values**

The ability to form attachments, reliability, social competence—these are among the most important fundamental values of humanity. We become socially competent when we have a healthy measure of self-confidence and security.

If the child knows that he is accepted in his existence and his abilities, then creativity, courage, self-trust, initiative and daring grow in him; the child can meaningfully meet demands and master difficulties. Such a child can also yield in conflict situations and forgive others; he knows how to wait his turn and is able to do without, to lose and to understand.

**Fostering Social Competency**

The development of social aptitude can be supported by the daily rhythm of the kindergarten; phases of full immersion in the group activities alternate with time when the child is allowed to be focused on himself and can follow his own intentions, for example, in free play. Phases of an active turning outward and phases of quiet listening and concentrated perception should harmoniously balance each other. Eating meals together is particularly valuable for developing social powers; the conscious cultivation of the eating activity extends far beyond customs and manners. Just as in many other activities, the example of the adults will make the difference between a merely formal or a heartfelt saying of grace, quiet consideration or nervous unrest, humor or pedantry, to name just a few examples. The children are guided unconsciously by these role models. The way in which adults treat each other—how they deal with force, which conflict resolution strategies they prefer, how much tolerance they can muster—has a strong impact and is mirrored in the child's behavior. Children learn through the realities they experience in daily life.

## 8. Media Competency in Kindergarten and Elementary School

Media competency is expected of an adult nowadays at a matter of course, just like everyone is expected to be able to use public transportation or to show appropriate behavior in traffic. But how do we acquire this competency? With traffic, for instance, no one would expect young children to be able to navigate in traffic; they would be completely overwhelmed. Before children can move independently in traffic, they must first have fully developed an array of sensori-motor faculties to be able to perform simultaneously all the tasks necessary. For instance, in order to ride a bicycle, one must be able to keep one's balance at all times without losing one's orientation, and, on top of that, be able to make an assessment of the traffic situation and react to it appropriately. The maturity of development that is necessary in this situation does not develop in traffic but through completely different activities and within a protected educational environment. The ADAC [the German equivalent of AAA] warns rightfully of the dangers of letting children get into street traffic on a bicycle on their own before the age of ten.

## Contact with Media

The same is true in regard to dealing with modern media. True media competency worthy of its name does not develop as a result of a use of media in early childhood, but by acquiring the entirely different faculties which must come first. The most important and fundamental of these is the development of the sensorimotor abilities necessary for the brain to gain its full level of achievement in the first place, and through which the organism gains the necessary stability to develop in a healthy way.

The child is existentially dependent on being afforded a widely differentiated development of the sense organs by ever again directly and actively experiencing the world in its abundance of qualitative sense impressions. For example, only in this way can a child experience the smell, taste, look, and sound of an object as qualities that belong together, as different sense modalities that coalesce into one, single object. It is a long learning process to develop through one's own inner activity the ability to build a meaningful connection from bits of information obtained via different sensory faculties and integrating their meaning. This ability forms the basis for thinking and discrimination; supported by this integrative ability we can later in life distill knowledge from data, meaning from symbols, and understanding from texts. It is precisely this faculty which must be initiated during the first years of childhood and which cannot be addressed through electronic media.

Computers and television actually reduce the sensory diversity and richness to the eye and ear and obliterate the congruence of image and sound perception, because the sounds emerging from the loudspeaker (for example, music or the voice of an unseen speaker) are coming from an entirely different realm of reality than what is visible on the screen. Moreover, sound and sight impressions are disconnected from physical activity, for the child's natural movement activity, to a high degree, is at a standstill during media use.

If we truly aim to design education with the child in mind, as the current educational plans stipulate, the laws of child development must be given the

consideration they deserve. It would be irresponsible, even just for physiological reasons, to make use of electronic media [television and computers] in preschool and kindergarten, because at that age the sense organs and the corresponding parts of the brain are not yet fully developed and matured, and all sensory impressions are still directly involved in developing the network of the brain itself. To argue that the content of such programs is valuable for children misses the mark completely. Brain researcher Manfred Spitzer remarks in this context, "A television, video or computer screen is harmful to the child, even if what is playing is the most fantastic children's program, the most beautiful animal movie, or the most intelligent learning program."

As much as Waldorf education values the subjects of media and computers in the upper grades and high school classroom, it is emphatically opposed to using electronic media as teaching tools in the kindergarten and elementary schools. To enable the older child to develop optimal media competency, the younger child must not be exposed to electronic media.

## Aspects of Developmental Psychology

Even if we ignore the physiological effects of electronic media, as most people do, and regard only the content aspect, Waldorf education sees no convincing reason for using media as teaching tools in kindergarten and elementary school. Enough studies have shown that children are not mature enough to process the content side of film productions. They are hardly able to understand the plot and context of a film and, most importantly, are unable to determine that what they are seeing is fiction. They accept the fiction as reality just as they accept the rest of their surroundings as reality; they perceive what is in the film to be as real as the rest of their environment. Only during elementary school years do the children slowly acquire the ability to differentiate between media fiction and reality, and even then few children are capable of organizing the string of events created by the film editing with any kind of capacity of thought. At about age twelve they are able to comprehend the production; however they still do not possess the adult capacity to distance themselves from the content of the film.

The advertising industry uses this knowledge of development to their advantage and targets children and youth. They know that at this age children believe the claims made in any advertisement to be the truth. At earliest around age twelve, the children begin to grasp that the intent of the advertisement is directed at them, and even then they still lack critical distance.

At the time of puberty when the capacity for reflective, conscious directing of one's own impulses actually has an organic foundation in the frontal lobe of the brain, only then has the young human being become developmentally able to enter into a conscious and independent critical examination of the media and their messages. And then he *should* begin to examine them, because now he is ready and equipped to apply his faculties successfully to the media—faculties, which he has developed through experiences in completely different realms of life. Foregoing the use of electronic media in early education is no disadvantage. To the contrary, it now proves to be a catalyst for developing superior media competency. The use of computers has been shown to be pedagogically counterproductive when it occurs too early during the first school years or even before school. In Israeli schools which work extensively with computers, studies have shown (2001) that computer-supported instruction did not bring about any improvement of the learning accomplishments even in math classes and, instead, set off a tendency to deterioration of learning.

As reasonable as it seems to work on the goal of guiding young human beings towards developing the complex action and thought sequences for using electronic media, the point in time when one begins such instruction is of critical importance. If the young child is prompted to deal with media before the maturing of organ-specific processes and of the brain's frontal lobes, not only does he not yet have the means to even attempt to meet this goal, but the ability to acquire this prerequisite is hindered, rendering the goal unattainable. Therefore, from the perspective of Waldorf education, instruction in electronic media should not begin until puberty.

# Capacities Developed in the Elementary School

## 9. Independence and Self-Reliance

Waldorf education relies on the fact that development does not proceed in linear fashion, but in stages of metamorphosis in which the later stage never appears to have come directly from the earlier stage, but rather in a step-by-step dynamic of polar transformation. The self-reliance of adolescents accordingly cannot be fostered by demanding it to be present already in the young child. Rather it requires that, first, fundamental powers are to be created and fostered on an entirely different level, which will later serve as nurturing ground for developing independence.

One of these fundamental powers is the faculty of imitation, which is still strongly present in a child throughout the first grades of school. Joyously, the child strives to imitate the teacher, who is able to do what the child as yet cannot do; the young child observes how the teacher skillfully and adeptly performs a task, and the urge rises in him to imitate such activities as precisely as possible. Thus, imitation leads gradually to self-reliance and independence. But the child pays close attention not only to activities which the teacher performs

but also to the teacher's inner attitude towards the task. Naturally, the teacher is accomplished in the tasks of writing, drawing and arithmetic. But with what precision and inner presence does he draw or write on the blackboard? How much is he as a person present in what

he does? Calm diligence and truthful, earnest effort make a deep impression on the child. Children are not primarily interested in results, but rather the way the results come about. It is the spirit in which the work is performed, the consciously executed gesture, which on one hand does justice to the task but, on the other hand and perhaps more importantly, serves as an expression of an artistic will to create form. The authority of the teacher begins here, not in rules and superior knowledge, and now, as ever before, the children seek this authority as an orientation and model for their own behavior.

When the school child develops the yearning to learn and do himself what the teacher modeled through work and attitude, this is the first step towards a well-formed, sustainable independence. A second key factor in the process of gaining self-reliance [autonomy] is the right timing, when the child has developed the impulse to practice on his own. Any challenge or demand from the outside can obstruct the development of this tender shoot, and often the first days and weeks in school determine whether an independent attitude towards learning will come about. Given an atmosphere of trust, imitation and devotion transform into the will to learn and joy of exploration.

# 10. Fostering Health through Rhythm

In a world of ever more ubiquitous technology, the structuring of our lives in a rhythmic way gains significance, not only for the well being of the child's soul, but also for his physical health and psychological development, as modern rhythm research confirms. In this respect, what is good for the kindergarten is also good for the elementary grades. Rhythmic order engenders reliability and stability; "un-rhythm" or lack of structure favors uncertainty, motor unrest, and lack of ordered thought, and, on a physical level it obstructs the consolidation of organ-specific rhythms such as the frequency of breath and pulse and intestinal peristalsis. Such instability can be prevented through establishing reliable yet flexible and lively rhythms.

**Rhythm in Class**

With these considerations in mind, it is a basic principle of Waldorf education to structure the daily classes according to rhythmic patterns. A two-hour block each morning is dedicated to starting the day together. This main lesson is organized in three parts which are connected through flowing transitions. The beginning phase is characterized by rhythmic-musical movement games and exercises together with singing, playing the recorders or other instruments, and reciting verses and poems or performing short

theatrical scenes. The teacher has the task in this phase to establish an inner rhythm [breath] between lively, stimulating movement sequences and quiet "inner centering." The individuality of each child is acknowledged and at the same time integrated into the common stream of the classroom community. There are many other rhythmic elements that could be named here, ranging from the cheerful and humorous to the earnest and serious.

The previous elements play a role in the second phase, the "work phase." The focus of this phase is teaching a particular subject every morning for a period of three to four weeks, the so-called block method of teaching. This organizational form allows the children to become deeply engrossed in one subject at a time: form drawing, writing, reading, arithmetic, and, later, the sciences, history and vocational fields such as construction, agriculture and handwork.

Curiosity, wonder, tension, excitement, and sometimes anxious anticipation—these all characterize the student's first encounter with a new topic. As his interest awakens, the student slowly becomes familiar with the new material. During the second week, the encounter intensifies, learning gains substance. Through eager grasping and practice, the student slowly comprehends the material, warms up to it and becomes enthusiastic, and also learns to work on it independently and creatively. In the third and fourth weeks the student gains overview and perspective. The student has reached a comprehensive understanding of the subject and developed new knowledge and faculties, which he now can "digest." The subject is laid to rest, to be resumed in another lesson block later. The student is allowed to "forget" what he has learned so that after some time has passed, it will be available to him in the form of new abilities.

The main lesson time closes harmoniously in the third phase of story telling. While the teacher is talking, bringing forth meaningful images before the inner eye of the child, an almost audible exhaling can be heard. During the work phase of the main lesson, the child employed all his powers, expended great energy in writing or reading, carefully drawing beautiful and difficult forms or doing arithmetic, but now he is immersed in a world of inner imagery and can let go of any restlessness and tension which may have occurred previously.

Just as each main lesson unit is thoroughly rhythmically structured, so is the continuum of days, weeks and months, yes, of the entire year organized in a rhythmic-dynamic way. Through the processes of breathing in, holding one's breath, compacting, and breathing out, the child can develop resonance in his soul and find his own rhythm.

## Structuring of Learning Steps

In structuring the sequence of learning steps, Waldorf education attends to keeping a certain rhythm, fully supported by modern sleep research. All learning is based upon a certain construction process. It begins with active familiarization and initial perception of the new material to be learned and continues into a second phase with bringing the subject matter into the immediate present or retrieving it from a distance of time. If we want the student to gain a solid hold of the subject and transform it into a faculty or skill, we need to interrupt the conscious learning activity and allow for sleep. Only in "forgetting" what he has learned, at least once or even several times, does the body of learning sink into the subconscious and a true absorption of and saturation with the subject matter is achieved. Accordingly, each lesson unit is ideally composed in a three-day rhythm. (Depending on circumstances, this can be accomplished in units of shorter duration.)

In the first step the child meets the new subject matter (class topic). At first, this encounter remains in the realm of becoming acquainted, of active awareness and shared reflection. The phenomenon, the observed fact is not yet subjected to interpretation, evaluation or definition. The following day brings the task of carefully remembering what the students observed and experienced the day before. Together the students develop a picture that is as comprehensive and clear as possible. The third day shows that the child has largely assimilated the subject matter at hand—first through outer, then inner contemplation, and in the "forgetting" that lies between—to such a degree that now he can work with it freely and independently.

Concepts which are developed in this manner are not grafted onto the child's mind, but remain full of life and can still grow. If through this guided three-step learning we afford the child sufficient time to internalize a subject, to perceive the essence of a subject, and to learn the fundamentals through practice, then he will develop a wealth of further possibilities that thematically follow the course of the lessons but are discovered very independently. The children will be easily motivated to join in the further development of the lessons through their own contributions and thus the three-phase method simultaneously contributes to the development of independence.

# 11. Movement Education

Movement and cognitive learning are closely connected. Many children today enter school with insufficient dexterity and motor-foot skills. Therefore Waldorf education gives wide latitude in the lesson plans for the first few grades for fostering the gross and fine motor skills. In kindergarten this process of motor development was stimulated and supported. Now in the elementary school it becomes a focus of morning practice. Running, jumping, hopping,

skipping, and, last but not least, stomping exercises for the feet are targeted consciously and integrated into the lessons. And since the feet are often still cold and stiff, they are even guided to "write" and "grasp" during play, for example, to make tracks in the sand. Too often the children are clumsy with their hands and lack the right skills. They are put through a lot of work in finger games and coordination exercises preparatory to more delicate tasks such as playing the recorder and knitting.

Once the joy of movement is awakened, the children cannot find an end to inventing ever-new games on their own. In the schoolyard they jump rope, ride unicycles, walk on stilts or juggle balls. In many schools circus troupes have formed in which many a child who initially appeared helpless achieve true mastery as an acrobat.

Gymnastics and physical education offer many more diverse opportunities for practice, and emphasis is given to the group aspect and playing by rules. Artistic exercises are especially useful for developing movement. Eurythmy is the prime example. After roughly the third grade most children can coordinate their movement sequences with aplomb and have gained in this process both inner and outer confidence.

## 12. Speech, Reading Skills, and Foreign Languages

Waldorf education thoroughly fosters the child's language competency throughout all his years in school. The soul life of the child becomes more and more differentiated in this process, because language not only serves to describe outer facts but is also a means of expression for inner processes and images. Therefore each main lesson offers the entire spectrum of language possibilities—from artistic, image-rich poetry and prose to the more sober, descriptive language of facts and concepts. Every day the class recites verses and poems and speaks or performs theatre scenes. At first this is done in chorus, so the children can quickly learn the piece by heart, and they slowly gain enough self-confidence through daily repetition to also be able to speak in front of a larger circle of people. The students practice precise diction that helps them learn to use language for concise, accurate description. As they mature, the children learn to use this factually oriented language for writing.

A third kind of encounter with language is experienced during the daily "story" portion of the lesson. The teacher tells stories that are oriented to the children's stage of development. With the poetic magic of inner imagery, he touches on the questions of life, some of which the children speak about, but some also remain as unexpressed questions within the children. Through repeated telling of these stories through the medium of language, the children learn to create their own inner images. This has a positive effect on their speaking ability as well as their emotional life. This process best unfolds if the teacher has prepared the storytelling so well that he can completely let go of reading from the book and tell the story freely, maintaining full eye contact with the children.

A lasting enhancement of the experience of language is achieved through instruction in two foreign languages. In German-speaking schools the children start in the first grade with English and French, or possibly Russian. The forces of imitation are still so strong at this age that the children just flow into the stream of the language through listening, singing, and playing. Foreign languages with their peculiar structures not only enrich the perceptive faculties of the child but they also provide for a richer and more differentiated range of verbal expression, down into gestures and movement expression.

During the last third of elementary school, speaking and listening skills are increasingly applied also in writing, and thus writing and reading competencies are developed. It is very important to allow each child to find the "right timing" so that language competency does not suffer attrition in writing. Some children excel at oral expression but may need more time to achieve the same confidence in their writing skills, and vice versa.

## 13. Education through Art

While artistic activities in kindergarten stimulate the expression of the child's creative powers and are subconsciously involved in forming the physical body, the pedagogy of the elementary school focuses on working with the forces of soul which have been freed-up and can now be consciously used by the child. In Waldorf education artistic activity is not limited to specific, separate classes, but permeates all lessons as a methodological principle. The child is challenged towards ever finer perception and creative form giving, so that he connects with the subject matter down into the realm of his will. For example, the child discovers the world of color through watercolor painting. The teacher directs the child in painting exercises that allow him to experience the qualities of color and their relationships. Training in the area of differentiated perception takes place which enables him to learn to differentiate nuances, gradations and qualities in many other areas as well.

Similarly with music, the effects are not limited to the music lessons. Tone, melody, and rhythm move the children's souls in manifold ways. The abilities to hear and listen, almost a lost art today, are cultivated, and in these processes of listening to outer sound, the child at the same time finds access to his inner life, to himself, and also to other human beings whom he joins in listening to and making music. When musical perception is successfully exercised, the child breathes differently and can even approach others in a more perceptive and inwardly vivid manner.

In this context, modeling with beeswax or clay takes on special importance. Forming these malleable materials trains the hands in touch and creation of form. It teaches a differentiated feeling for space and fine motor skills. The form-giving faculties of the child, which so far (up to the change of teeth) were actively engaged in building his organs, are now available to the child, not only as creative forces, but also as forces for thinking. Through working with his hands, the child can connect with the natural process of becoming. Art opens the door to creativity.

Form drawing is introduced and developed during the first four years of school in a structured artistic approach. The child learns to make precise drawings of regular forms, at first simple ones developed from the polarity of straight and curved lines; then more difficult and challenging forms, increasing step-by-step. The sense of form is challenged in most differentiated ways through lines which cross in regular intervals, mirror each other or even invert. By going through the complex process of form drawing and the discovery of new and ever-new inventions of forms, the child gains a power of orientation which can lead to a sense of certitude that reaches far into his thought processes and his sense of self. At the same time he becomes intuitively aware of the formative forces and the laws of form which constitute the world.

Eurythmy is an art form that moves and vitalizes the whole being. Children experience in this class how they can integrate into the movement of body and limbs all the faculties of soul and spirit acquired so far, following objective laws. For example, the forms that a child creates in form drawing with paper and pencil, initially as mere imitation and increasingly freer and more creative, can be experienced in eurythmy with the whole being. The child learns about the various qualities of physical space. These qualities of movement in eurythmy are connected with the experience of the musical elements of tone, melody, and harmony, and also with the powerful expression found in the elements of speech: vowels and consonants, syntax and poetic imagery.

# 14. Introduction to Mathematics

Beginning lessons in mathematics in the Waldorf elementary school are based on rhythmically structured movement processes. Counting is learned by speaking in chorus, accompanied by rhythmic stomping, clapping, skipping and jumping in unison. For example, the path to the times tables emerges when every second or third number is emphasized, again accompanied by a certain movement sequence or an omitted movement sequence. This requires much concentration and eye-hand coordination.

The teacher makes sure that over time the movements become less and less pronounced, so the children transition gradually from limb-supported recitation to simply speaking the times tables, and conscious internal management takes the place of outer activity. As the children first assimilate the multiplication tables and the number field up to 100, through physical and sensorimotor activity, they prepare the ground on which later the purely mental mathematical computations can unfold smoothly. Counting and calculating are connected to their own activity, and, for example, the process of multiplication is simply a higher level of counting.

In applying multiplication in a practical manner, the child experiences the meaningful connection between the world of numbers and occurrences of everyday life. Numbers are something real that we can interact with inwardly and outwardly.

Another essential aspect of Waldorf education concerns the principle of always starting from the whole and moving to the parts. For example, the children are guided to handle the first arithmetic operation as the additive

analysis of a number: 12 = 7 + 5 or 6 + 4 + 2, and so forth. This method gives the child the basic understanding that many paths can lead to the same result. This keeps their thinking flexible and has a positive effect on social interaction, in that one will recognize the path of the other as being as equally viable as one's own.

But this method engenders further, more profound effects. It is of no small importance to the child's later attitude toward the world that in the early grades arithmetic is taught to proceed from the whole to the parts, instead of from the parts to the whole, which is how it is usually taught. Since children experience things very concretely and they connect the numbers with realities, it makes a very big difference whether one is accustomed to starting from the whole and then going into the separate parts, or whether one views the world as a collection of parts that must be added together. The social and ecological attitudes in later life will also be very different if the faculty has been well developed for considering the whole, with a part of it shared by all human beings, instead of just thinking of one's own part.

## 15. Ethical and Moral Values

To create a basis for consciousness of ethical and moral values during the elementary school years, Waldorf education does not set about specific discussions of ethical-moral issues during the lessons. Rather it tries to involve

the student in experiences of awe, respect, love and gratitude through the way the subjects are taught.

For this approach to succeed, these faculties must be authentically present in the adults who influence the children through example. In that case, the children will also come to deep feelings of awe, gratitude, and love in their encounters with nature, for example, or in perceiving the primal images found in fairy tales, fables, and stories. They will develop growing awareness in their encounters with the world and with other people. The groundwork for such possibilities of experience is carefully cultivated during the lessons in school so that the children can find their own way. If these values unfold freely from within the child, then, over the years, that sense of responsibility and duty towards the world and other human beings takes form which includes the readiness to help and act on behalf of others.

# The Education and Self-Education of the Educator

Teachers and educators in the Waldorf schools can realize their educational goals only if certain social and organizational conditions are also present, through which the quality of the pedagogical work is safeguarded, both within and without. Unless otherwise noted these conditions apply equally to the kindergarten and elementary school.

## 1. Self-Education as the Foundation for Action

The encounter between adult and child forms the core of all education. It is the adult's responsibility to form this encounter and render it fruitful, and he can fulfill this task only to the degree that he furthers his own personality development. Self-education of the adult in support of his/her modeling function is one of the cornerstones of education and learning processes.

Self-education includes the core task to change habits out of one's own free will. The adult can accomplish this task through his own motivation, but he can also find exterior incentives and support. Since the founding of Waldorf education, its philosophical foundation has included a canon of writings which should be explored in meditation and are suited to help deepen one's pedagogical work. An important aid in finding a supportive, inner connection with the children is also the daily ritual of reviewing the day, not in the sense of mirroring one's own self, but rather through an intense perception of what was experienced with the children and in one's own behavior on that particular day. It is the prerequisite and, at the same time, the goal of Waldorf pedagogy to understand education and learning processes as a systemic task. In other words, all questions relating to the children and their development are simultaneously always questions relating to the educator himself, how he can change in order to give the children a corresponding and appropriate space for development.

## Joy and Competency in Practical Work

It is the task of the teachers to perform many different kinds of work, be it housework or

handicrafts, and to guide the children towards acquiring certain dexterous skills and cognitive processes not through a teaching presentation but in such a way that the work tasks emerge quite naturally, factually and logically to meet the necessities of day-to-day life. Their educational value lies in the fact that the child meets them as facts of life and will wish to imitate.

The educator will need a repertoire of practical skills for this purpose, extending from homemaking to certain handicrafts, some workshop skills with tools, and, depending on the circumstances, garden work or basic animal husbandry. If the teachers are enthusiastically striving to acquire the necessary practical competencies that allow them to fulfill the tasks at hand, then the children will in turn be encouraged to engage in creative activities which they will unfold in the world of play as corresponds to their age. The educational goal of a feeling of coherence can be built up in this manner as a lasting quality of the personality.

In the lower grades the same quality of education and learning develops if the teacher is connected in such a way with the subject matter he teaches that he can present it as an artistic, exemplary image of the realities of this world and mankind. Such images touch the children's feelings and create a relationship with the world, which unfolds lasting effect as a foundational experience of coherence. The prerequisite for this effect is the teacher's level of interest and immersion in the subject matters he teaches. (Rudolf Steiner demonstrated just how far this interest may reach when he suggested that introductory arithmetic should always start with the result, for example, from the sum instead of the addend, and connects this suggestion with the deepest questions of human realization, such as those which Kant addresses when he speaks of "synthetic judgments a priori.")

**Artistic Competency**

Artistic activities are a part of life in Waldorf education. This is especially true in the kindergarten. These activities include watercolor painting, drawing with colored beeswax block crayons, modeling with beeswax, singing, playing music on simple instruments, rhythmic speaking, finger and hand games, movement games, and the special movement activity of eurythmy. All of these activities are integrated into a daily and weekly schedule in such a way that they build a rhythmic whole without particular learning goals or mental processing of what happens [during the day] with the children. Instead, the teacher is there to be an example for the children. Whether or not the artistic elements in the children's daily routines become an effective educational force depends upon the teacher's efforts at the appropriate skill level and his creative will.

The Waldorf elementary school curriculum includes artistic classes starting in first grade. In the lower grades singing, simple instrumental play, speaking in chorus, movement, painting, drawing and sculpting generally fall under the guidance [tasks] of the class teacher. Furthermore, the class teacher is responsible—together with the track class teachers—to imbue all instruction with an artistic focus. Especially the rhythmic composition of the class instruction as a basic element of a true "art of education" presupposes a fine sense for the vital and soul disposition of the student and requires forms of practice and training that correspond to that disposition.

But artistic competency of yet a completely different nature is required of the kindergarten and elementary school teacher, namely in the social realm, in direct contact with the children. The teacher must possess a high measure of sensitivity and empathy, presence of mind and intuition so that he can meet the children, to learn from them while at the same time helping them in their education. These are faculties that can be developed through self-education, in particular through artistic practice.

# 2. Professional and Continuing Education

The Waldorf teacher's faculties require appropriate professional and continuing education. Working responsibly in Waldorf education requires basic training either at Waldorf teacher training seminars or in qualifying courses which provide training for those already practicing in other professions or who have a degree in some other field. Some teacher training courses are scheduled such to allow a teacher to continue working while taking the course. These courses are equal to the full-time training courses in content and scope.

Anthropological theory of knowledge and child development studies are at the center of all Waldorf teacher training. These studies contribute to the deepening of one's own worldview as well as to becoming familiar with the foundations of Waldorf education, its basis, curriculum and classroom methods. The qualifying training steps also involve a relatively long internship, in the course of which the student teacher plans, designs and reflects upon his own pedagogical intentions and actions.

Indispensable for working in the Waldorf educational system is regular attendance in continuing education courses in the arts and sciences, on current childhood issues, and on methodological and didactic topics. Of equal importance is the regular participation of all Waldorf educators in conferences, which will be outlined in the next chapter.

The basic professional education courses in the kindergarten and elementary school areas, just like the qualifying professional training and continuing education courses, are subject to certain differences in organizational structure. This is a result of the varying constraints that are set by the respective state departments of education and supervising agencies in regard to issuing teaching, kindergarten directorship and group child care licenses.

# 3. Working Together

Fruitful cooperation between adults is an essential element for the success of any educational work with the children. Cultivating this cooperation is a key endeavor for the individuals and organizations working in the field of Waldorf education. The following organizational forms are in place to provide for this cooperative element.

## Weekly Faculty Meeting and Child Study

In general, the faculty at a Waldorf school meet once a week in a conference work session. At these meetings issues of administration and self-governance within the school are discussed as well as imminent organizational tasks; however the primary focus is the work on pedagogical issues. Themes such as developmental psychology and anthropology are studied, providing the participants further training in these areas. The weekly conference also includes methodical discussions of individual children in relation to pedagogical questions of issue at the time. The goal of these discussions is not to form any kind of judgment about a particular child, but rather to get nearer to the essence of the child and gain a detailed understanding of his or her developmental situation in consideration of all the anthropological, medical, and social conditions that are present, in order to arrive at providing appropriate help.

## Working with Parents

Giving due consideration to the uniqueness of each child means working with those who are closest to the child, namely the parents. In an atmosphere of complete respect for each other's pedagogical competence, an exchange of information about the child at home and at school can take place. Everyone fulfilling a pedagogical function claims the privilege of being allowed to develop his own unique relationship to the child in utter freedom. Therefore it is necessary for parents and teachers to refrain from trying to issue directions or imposing their will on each other—directly or indirectly.

Rather, it is of importance to share with each other what they experience with the child and to enter a dialogue about the pedagogical approach of one's own work. Such regular conversations are held between teachers and individual parents (parent-teacher conferences) and all parents of a child's group or class (parent meetings). They usually take place on the school premises but at times also at the parents'  home, which allows the teacher the opportunity to experience the child's home environment. This ensures that the parents and pedagogical staff are always in communication and informed about each child's situation and that there is the highest possible clarity.

The school's inherent tendency to maintain a distance is overcome and diverse opinions about educational questions can exist side by side, without engendering uncertainty or confrontational tension in the child. On the contrary, the child sees a model for how in the social realm differing concepts can complement each other harmoniously and be supportive of each other. Moreover, this process creates a basis for unembellished exchange of real experiences and to thus cultivate the principle of truthfulness.

Further opportunities for parents and teachers to work together come about through the preparation of festivals and bazaars, through initiatives around public events and through the co-responsible participation of parents and teachers in the various committees of a kindergarten or school. Every Waldorf school finds its own organizational forms for cooperative activity between parents and teachers for the good of the school and its students.

# 4. Cooperation between Kindergarten and Grade School

Human development is a continuum; it knows no boundaries between elementary and middle school grades, between preschool, school age and young adulthood. The greater the holistic view of the developmental years, the more appropriate it is to the growing human being. For this reason Waldorf education sees as one of its tasks understanding the kindergarten and school as a single organismic whole that functions cooperatively.

This cooperation proceeds on various levels. When the kindergarten and school share the same space facilities, then the teachers are together regularly at the weekly pedagogical conference. The child's transition from kindergarten into school can be carefully monitored from both sides. The first grade teacher tries to get as detailed a picture as possible of all the children he is accepting into the class through comprehensive discussions with the kindergarten teacher, who also makes all written records available. This shared experience of the child, as well as joint discussions with the parents, forms the basis for a consciously structured transition into school appropriate for each individual child.

When the kindergarten and school are administratively connected as well, or working under joint public agency supervision, there is naturally broader cooperation, including legal-economic requirements. However, many Waldorf kindergartens exist independently of any school. In these cases there are varying degrees of cooperation between the kindergarten and neighboring schools, but the transition between kindergarten and school is still a path with shared responsibilities. Even in cases where the child is going from a Waldorf kindergarten into a public or parochial school, the Waldorf teacher makes a special effort to contact colleagues and administrators of the new school so that, together with the parents, an optimal situation is created for the child.

# 5. Cooperation with Therapists, Doctors, and Expert Consultants

Today childhood development progresses much faster that in former years, and the stages of child development generally recognized in conventional developmental psychology can often no longer be clearly discerned. The line between individual signatures of behavior and behavioral problems, that is, behavior that requires special attention and monitoring, has become blurred. That is why Waldorf schools make an effort to work with physicians and therapists on a continuing basis. Their professional opinions are of significant support in the educational and formative processes of individual children and help teachers and parents understand the uniqueness of each individual child.

Educators working in a Waldorf kindergarten also have access to competent, regionally organized expert consultation that covers direct pedagogical and methodological/didactic issues and extends also to conceptual and organizational questions. Some expert consultants are hired directly into the schools; others fulfill this task aside from their regular practices. In either case they are experienced pedagogical experts with a close connection to practical educational and teaching issues.

Similarly, experienced teachers who have worked for a long time, and often are still working, in Waldorf schools are extending consultation and advisory accompaniment to colleagues through continuing education courses in many areas, through taking an active part in professional conventions, and through mentorship situations within their own schools and other schools as well. In a number of cases there are also pertinent courses being offered through the regional working groups of the Waldorf schools, and colleagues are assigned to special tasks within these groups.

# 6. Research and Quality Development

## Documenting the Development of the Children

A Waldorf kindergarten keeps written documentation of the experiences the children have while in their care. This documentation serves to support the teachers' own awareness and also to form a basis for discussions with the parents, colleagues and teachers of schools which the child may later attend. Furthermore, protocols are kept covering the child studies by the college of teachers. The documentation may be written in a standardized format of notes in a notebook template which has been developed by the Association of Waldorf Kindergartens and is frequently updated, or the teacher may record the experiences of the individual children in a format of his own design. The file will also contain a collection of the child's drawings and watercolor paintings, which are then given to the parents either at the end of the school year or when the child leaves the kindergarten.

When the child enters a Waldorf school, he or she undergoes a thorough examination to determine the status of his health and development, and the results are discussed with the parents. At the end of the first and subsequent school years, the parents of each child receive a detailed report. This is not a grades report, but an extensive evaluation in which the instructing teachers characterize the learning behavior of the child, the progress the child made in the course of the school year, and indications about steps still be taken. During the early school years, the report is primarily an orientation for the parents, but it is also addressing the child himself.

## Research in Pedagogical Work

Waldorf education highly values a certain degree of research activity that the teachers show within their fields of expertise. Such research by nature is subject to very different conditions than usual. The principle of objective distance between research subject and researcher, who must not influence the processes under consideration, can have no validity here. Children do show their unique character only within a certain type of human relationship. Therefore research that is relevant to educational practice happens primarily in a real, responsive educational process itself.

Waldorf educators in kindergarten and elementary school regularly reflect upon the perceptions and observations of their daily pedagogical activities, exchange and discuss the findings with their colleagues within a larger framework (professional and regional conferences, for example), and document those results, so they can ever-new account for the foundations of their work. A variety of existing publications make available to the public such research findings and conceptual suggestions, for example, the magazines *Erziehungskunst* [Art of Education], *Medizinisch-Pädagogische Konferenz* [Medical-Pedagogical Conference], and the internal *Lehrerrundbrief* [Newsletter for Teachers].

More comprehensive presentations are made available through the Waldorf Kindergarten Association, the Association of Free Waldorf Schools, and their research and information departments in the form of brochures, workbooks, classroom materials and books. Moreover, various publishing houses offer numerous fundamental writings on all areas of Waldorf education, which inventory is continuously supplemented with new releases.

## Intention and Quality Standards

Anthroposophy is the common foundation for all Waldorf schools, but the actual structure of every school is different and in a continuous process of development. That is why, when addressing quality standards, every Waldorf school should not only review and describe its pedagogical concept and the organizational forms resulting from it, but should also continually adapt its concept and forms to its ever-present needs. This happens as a matter of course by methodical work on a mission statement during the formative process, whereby all active, accountable members of the organization—faculty, parents, agencies and supporters from the greater community—participate to ensure the present needs and questions will find their way into the process. Whether a kindergarten or school will get outside help with quality management or undergo external certification is an individual decision.

Waldorf schools generally implement quality assurance by regularly extending conscious awareness and evaluation to the various processes in the school and by redesigning them if need be. One cannot fixate and thus assure pedagogical and social quality. Such quality is safeguarded only through binding procedures which periodically question the tasks and the conditions for work and education; similarly these procedures must allow for the possibility of new approaches.

Rudolf Steiner expressed the thought in his "fundamental sociological law" that in our time the communities and institutions no longer face the task, as in former times, of giving orientation to human beings as a group; to the contrary, they must serve the developmental needs of the individual human being. The underlying intention in forming a school is to create a living organism which can serve the developmental needs of the human being instead of preparing the individual to fit into a rigid framework. Waldorf schools and kindergartens take that into account by ever and again aligning their conceptual approach with the concrete educational and formative needs of the human beings involved.

## 7. Self-Governance

Since Waldorf education was founded in 1919, their system of cooperative self-management has been a special characteristic of their institutions. Together with those responsible for the legal and economic aspects, the faculty administer the school, attending to the planning and implementation of all necessary tasks, and there is no directive hierarchy within the staff members. While the school may be legally required to designate certain people as fulfilling leadership functions, the principle of cooperative self-government is nevertheless operative in actual practice. In the conference meetings, all involved parties strive constantly to form consensus of the tasks at hand and, on that basis, to develop guidelines for action. Individual colleagues or groups of colleagues implement the recommendations and decisions through specific mandates from the group work.

The model of collegial self-governance serves two main purposes, subtly connected with the quality of pedagogical work. For one, choosing an alternate organizational form rather than a rigid hierarchy among colleagues creates an atmosphere of positive interpersonal relationships based on mutual recognition and appreciation. A climate for true encounter develops, forming a basis for openness and honesty among colleagues in their interactions with each other and makes it possible to confidently delegate tasks to each other. Further, the principle of cooperative self-management sharpens one's awareness of the conditions and consequences of one's own work. No one can fall back on predetermined general conditions; everyone is responsible. Indeed, one can only arrive at truly free pedagogical decisions if the conditional constraints are expertly considered.

Through responsible self-management, a third goal is achieved, that of creating a real life situation for the children in which tolerance, personal initiative, responsibility, and productive cooperation are not only pretty words but are truly lived reality and social fact. This has a deep pedagogical effect on their own development into free, self-directed personalities.

## Responsible and Entrepreneurial Attitude

Children, especially young children, do not orient themselves on verbal instruction, but on the realities they live with in their environment. This includes the efforts made by those responsible in making the kindergarten or classroom a space for living, which they have created authentically, with much personal engagement. An attitude of "working per instructions" does not allow a situation to be genuine. Rather, the Waldorf kindergarten and school become partly one's "own enterprise." Entrepreneurial spirit is required. However, this step cannot be formulated or demanded. It is rather a question of attitude, just as the impulse for Waldorf education can thrive only upon the foundation of freedom of development.

## Managing the Organization

The Waldorf schools in Germany are for the most part organized along the association model, with a board of directors that carries the legal and financial responsibility for the school on an equal level with the college of teachers. The board is elected from members of the association and is responsible for finances, construction and maintenance of the building(s), business management, and representation of the organization to public authorities. As in the teachers college, the large amount of work is divided among delegates and committees who are given the necessary decision-making authority, time, and financial parameters to fulfill certain tasks.

Every Waldorf organization makes its own bylaws and, together with the parents, develops its own profile. One example of the legal structure of Waldorf schools is that the college of teachers, or a body that has been formed from the college of teachers to administer the school, has the sole authority to hire and dismiss teachers. However, they have an obligation to provide information to the board about these activities. On the whole, healthy communication between the various managing bodies is of great significance to the success of the social process.

**Cooperation among Waldorf Institutions**

In spite of their autonomy, no Waldorf school works in isolation, but rather in association with other Waldorf organizations. The Waldorf kindergarten movement has its own regional and national associations (such as the Waldorf Kindergarten Association in Germany) and the International Association for Steiner/Waldorf Early Childhood Education. Waldorf schools also have regional and national associations such as AWSNA in North America and the Bund in Germany. The name "Waldorf" is legally protected by trademark law and is only granted to institutions that have successfully completed a thorough process of examination and can demonstrate a convincing concept backed by appropriately qualified pedagogical professionals. Newly founded schools are supported in the process of establishing themselves through mentor partnerships with established schools.

## 8. Integration into the Social Environment

In keeping with the principles of educational diversity and constitutionally mandated pluralism, Waldorf schools enrich the landscape of available educational institutions in a community or region. They take seriously the fact that they are a part of a living and evolving social architecture of interested parents and other members of the community. Meetings with neighboring representatives of different pedagogic orientations and with committees and groups on community and county levels not only open up opportunities for cooperation and coordination, but they allow for more clearly communicating one's own pedagogical concepts to the public. Almost every Waldorf school carries on an intensive public outreach program. Lectures, concerts, seminars, art courses, celebrations of seasonal festivals, open house days, and bazaars are some of the events, so that Waldorf schools become more or less active and significant co-creators of the community's cultural life.

# 9. Architecture and Space Design

Spaces and buildings are like an extended skin. Life happens in them, and their character has influence on the social processes, experiences and health of children. Therefore the design of the physical space for a kindergarten or elementary school should be according to principles that are not limited to functional criteria, but which help create an environment for the child with his enormous sensitivity that offers stimulation as well as a calming, comforting effect, fostering both security and openness. At the root of this approach is the knowledge of the effects generated by all details of color design, qualities of form and materials of furniture and accessories, choice of pictures, lighting, and so forth. These effects reach down into the physiological life processes.

The child should find himself in a well-structured environment, directly engaging his life awareness and far removed from indoctrination intent or pragmatic purposes, in an environment that in itself has formative powers. If a new building is an option, these factors come into play when designing the architectural features of the house. While rectangular-shaped rooms may be of functional appeal, an organic way of building that is free of the dictate of the right angle offers the possibility of creating rooms which give the young child

*Linden Hall, Sacramento Waldorf School, CA*

a much stronger life-awareness of being sheltered and held. Thus architecture can support the educational principles and simultaneously make them visible in the world.

*Kindergarten, Summerfield Waldorf School, CA*

*Lower grades classroom, Germany*

*The Waldorf School on the Roaring Fork, CO*

*Auditorium, the Waldorf School on the Roaring Fork, CO*

*The Toronto Waldorf School, Canada*

*The Pine Hill Waldorf School, NH*

# Bibliography

Ainsworth, M.D., M.C. Blehar, E. Waters and S. Wall. *Patterns of Attachment. A Psychological Study of the Strange Situation,* New York: 1978.

Antonovsky, Aaron. "Gesundheitsforschung versus Krankheitsforschung" ["Health Research vs. Disease Research"] in: A. Franke/M. Broda (Eds.): *Psychosomatische Gesundheit,* Tübingen: pp. 3–4, 1993.

_____. *Salutogenese. Zur Entmystifizierung der Gesundheit* [*Salutogenetics: Towards Demystifying Health*], Deutsche erweiterte Herausgabe von A. Franke, Tübingen: 1997.

Bellenberg, Gabriele. *Individuelle Schulliaufbahnen: Eine empirische Untersuchung über Bildungsverläufe von der Einschulung bis zum Abschluss* [*Individual School Careers: An Empirical Study of Education from the Start of School to Graduation*], Weinheim: 1999.

Bowlby, John and Mary D. Ainsworth (Eds.). *Deprivation of Maternal Care,* New York: 1966.

Eliot, Lise. *Was geht da drinnen vor? Die Gehirnentwicklung in den ersten fünf Lebensjahren* [*What Is Happening in There? The Development of the Brain in the First Five Years of Life*] (Deutsche Übersetzung [German Translation]), Berlin: 2001.

Grossarth-Matieek, Ronald. *Systemische Epidemiologie und präventive Verhaltensmedizin chronischer Erkrankungen. Strategien zur Aufrechterhaltung der Gesundheit* [*Systematic Epidemiology and Preventive Behavioral Medicine of Chronic Diseases. Strategies for Health Maintenance*], Berlin, New York: 1999.

Hildebrandt, Gunther, Maximilian Moser and Michael Lehofer. *Chronobiologie und Chronomedizin. Biologische Rhythmen—Medizinische Konsequenzen* [*Chronobiology and Chronomedicine. Biological Rhythms— Medical Consequences*], Stuttgart: 1998.

Hüther, Gerald. *Bedienungsanleitung für ein menschliches Gehirn* [*User Manual for the Human Brain*], Göttingen: 2001.

_____. "Wohin? Wofür? Weshalb? Über die Bedeutung innerer Leitbilder für die Hirnentwicklung" ["Where to? For What? Why? About the Importance of Inner Guiding Imagery for Brain Development"] in Gebauer and Hüther (Eds.). *Kinder suchen Orientierung. Anregungen für eine sinn-stiftende Erziehung* [*Children Are Looking for Direction. Suggestions for an Education that Engenders Meaning*], Düsseldorf, Zürich: 2002.

Kranich, Ernst-Michael. *Anthropologische Grundlagen der Waldorfpädagogik* [*Anthropological Foundations of Waldorf Pedagogy*], Stuttgart: 1999.

Largo, Remo. *Kinderjahre. Die Individualität des Kindes als erzieherische Herausforderung* [*The Individuality of Children as an Educational Challenge*], München: 2004.

Leber, Stefan. *Der Schlaf und seine Bedeutung. Geisteswissenschaftliche Dimensionen des Un- und Überbewussten* [*Sleep and Its Meaning. Spiritual-Science Dimensions of Un- and Superconsciousness*], Stuttgart: 1996.

Oerter, Rolf and Leo Montada (Eds.). *Entwicklungspsychologie* [*Developmental Psychology*], Weinheim, Basel, Berlin: 5. Auflage, 2002.

Opp, Günther, Michael Fingerle and Andreas Freytag (Eds.). *Was Kinder stärkt. Erziehung zwischen Risiko und Resilienz* [*What Makes Children Stronger: Education between Risk and Resilience*], München, Basel: 1999.

Patzlaff, Rainer. *Der gefrorene Blick. Physiologische Wirkungen des Fernsehens und die Entwicklung des Kindes* [*The Frozen View. Physiological Effects of Television and Child Development*], Stuttgart: 3. Auflage, 2004.

Piaget, Jean and B. Inhelder. *Die Psychologie des Kindes* [*Child Psychology*], Olten: 1973.

Richter, Tobias. *Pädagogischer Auftrag und Unterrichtsziele—vom Lehrplan der Waldorfschule* [*Educational Mandate and Teaching Goals—About the Waldorf School Curriculum*], Stuttgart: 2003.

Rittelmeyer, Christian. *Schulbauten positiv gestalten. Wie Schüler Farben und Formen erleben* [*Creating Positive School Buildings. How Students Experience Colors and Forms*], Wiesbaden, Berlin: 1994.

———. *Pädagogische Anthropologie des Leibes. Biologische Voraussetzungen der Erziehung und Bildung* [*Pedagogical Anthropology of the Body. Biological Foundations of Education*], Weinheim, München: 2002.

Schad, Wolfgang. "Die Idee der Evolution in der Pädagogik" ["The Idea of Evolution in Pedagogy"] in: *Erziehungskunst* 9, pp. 931–942, 2004.

Schäfer, Gerd E. (Ed.) *Bildung beginnt mit der Geburt. Ein offener Bildungsplan für Kindertageseinrichtungen in Nordrhein-Westfalen* [*Education Begins with Birth. An Open Curriculum for Childcare Centers in North Rhine Westphalia*], Weinheim, Basel: 2. Auflage, 2004.

Schuberth, Ernst. *Der Anfangsunterricht in der Mathematik an Waldorfschulen. Aufbau, fachliche Grundlagen und menschenkundliche Gesichtspunkte* [*The First Math Class in Waldorf Schools. Structure, Foundations and Human Science Views*], Stuttgart: 2. Auflage, 2001.

Schüffel, Wolfram, et al. (Eds.) *Handbuch der Salutogenese. Konzept und Praxis* [*Handbook of Salutogenesis. Concept and Application*] Gesellschaft München, Göttingen: pp. 431–439, 1998.

Spangler, Gottfried, et al. *Bindungstheorie: Stand der Forschung, neuere Entwicklungen und künftige Perspektiven* [*Attachment Theory: Review of Scientific Research, Newer Developments and Future Perspectives*] in: Heinz Mandl (Ed.). Bericht über den 40. Kongress der Deutschen Gesellschaft für Psychologie in München pp. 431–439, Göttingen: 1996.

Spitzer, Manfred. *Lernen. Gehirnforschung und die Schule des Lebens* [*Learning: Brain Research and the School of Life*], Heidelberg, Berlin: 2002.

———. *Vorsicht Bildschirm! Elektronische Medien, Gehirnentwicklung, Gesundheit und Gesellschaft* [*Caution: Television! Electronic Media, Brain Development, Health and Society*], Stuttgart, Düsseldorf, Leipzig: 2005.

Steiner, Rudolf. *Allgemeine Menschenkunde als Grundlage der Pädagogik* [*Foundations of Human Experience*], 14 Vorträge, Dornach: 9. Auflage, 1992.

———. *Die Erziehung des Kindes vom Gesichtspunkte der Geisteswissenschaft* [*Education of the Child in the Light of Spiritual Science*], Dornach: 2003.

———. *Erziehungs-, Unterrichts- und praktische Lebensfragen vom Gesichtspunkt anthroposophischer Geisteswissenschaft* [*Issues in Education, Teaching and Practical Life*], Vortrag vom 24.2.1921, in Rudolf-Steiner-Gesamtausgabe Band 297a, Dornach: 1998.

———. *Die gesunde Entwicklung des Menschenwesens. Eine Einführung in die anthroposophische Pädagogik und Didaktik* [*The Healthy Development of the Human Being: An Introduction to Anthroposophical Pedagogy and Didactics*], 16 Vorträge, Dornach: 4. Auflage, 1987.